Outlaw Tales
of Missouri

True Stories of the Show Me State's Most Infamous Crooks, Culprits, and Cutthroats

Second Edition

Sean McLachlan

TWODOT®

GUILFORD, CONNECTICUT
HELENA, MONTANA

AN IMPRINT OF GLOBE PEQUOT PRESS

To buy books in quantity for corporate use
or incentives, call **(800) 962-0973**
or e-mail **premiums@GlobePequot.com.**

A · T W O D O T® · B O O K

Layout: Adam Caporiccio
Project editor: Staci Zacharski
Map: Daniel Lloyd © 2014 Morris Book Publishing, LLC

Library of Congress Cataloging-in-Publication data is available on file.

ISBN 978-0-7627-9396-9

Printed in the United States of America

10 9 8 7 6 5 4 3 2 1

For Almudena, my wife, and Julián, my son

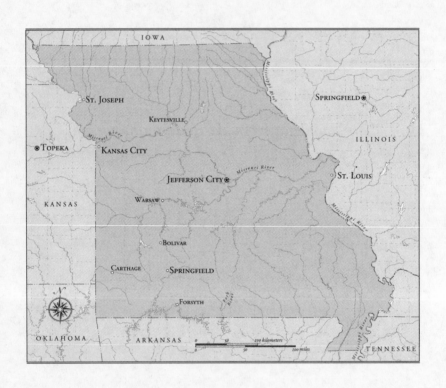

Contents

Acknowledgments

The work of many researchers, both professionals and dedicated amateurs, has gone into this book. I would especially like to thank the staff of the State Historical Society of Missouri in Columbia for help sifting through their vast collection of newspapers, books, and journals, and for their patience in answering what must have seemed an unending stream of questions. I would also like to thank Chris and Caitlin Lenon-Davis for providing a place of refuge for a wandering writer. A very special thank-you goes out to my wife, Almudena, for putting up with me disappearing for long periods of time into a pile of notes and papers, and my son, Julián, who was a very good kid while I wrote about very bad adults. This book is dedicated to them.

Introduction

When it comes to crime, Missourians never seem to do anything by half measures. Instead of an ordinary shootout with police, Missouri was the scene of one of the deadliest days in police history. Not content with being embroiled in a bloody Civil War, Missouri plunged into a bitter guerrilla conflict that started seven years earlier and ended two decades later than the war the rest of the country experienced. The average everyday gunman wasn't good enough for Missouri; it had to produce Jesse James and Cole Younger. It's no wonder that in the nineteenth century people used to call Missouri the "Outlaw State."

These are fourteen tales of Missouri's most famous criminals mixed in with some not so famous. In two well-known cases, Jesse James and Tom Pendergast, the focus is on their older brothers, Frank and Jim. Frank James led his brother in all things: He was the first to go to war, the first to become an outlaw, and the first to see the sense of getting out of the bank- and train-robbing business. It saved his life. Jim Pendergast created the Kansas City political machine that his younger brother Tom made famous. Jim taught Tom everything he knew, although Tom went on to learn considerably more.

One tricky thing with writing about outlaws is cutting through the generations of mythology that have grown up around them. Personalities such as Belle Starr became legends in their own time, with writers eagerly making up stories about her exploits to sell copy. Even when we get back to the original sources we find large parts of the story are told only by the outlaws themselves, the very people who have every reason to bend the truth. So when reading this book, as with reading any history book, it's best to keep a constant "maybe" stuck in the back of your mind. These stories are how it *probably* happened, judging from the best evidence . . .

. . . and the best evidence isn't always pretty. While everyone refers to Frank and Jesse James as the "James boys," as if they are the kids next door who mow your lawn, the facts show they could be ruthless killers, although they had a flair for the dramatic and performed occasional acts of chivalry that helped create their legend. Similarly, Belle Starr may not have been a glamorous outlaw, but rather a woman with terribly bad taste in men. And then, of course, there were the vicious vigilante wars of the Ozarks, where it became impossible to tell the criminals from the vigilantes. Granted, gunfights and bank robberies are exciting stuff, but crime is often ugly, and those who commit it usually have an ugly end.

So here they are, warts and all, some of the most daring and despicable Missourians who ever lived.

The Yocum Dollar
Counterfeit Currency
Worth More than the Real Thing

Four brothers hunched over a small furnace. Each wore the rough homespun of early frontiersmen and kept their muskets close at hand in case they were disturbed. The roaring flames made their shadows dance along the cave walls. One kept looking toward the cave entrance to make sure they weren't seen as another pulled out a pile of US government silver coins from a pouch. He dropped them into a pan, stuck the pan into the furnace, and waited. As soon as they had melted, another brother pulled out the pan and carefully poured the liquid silver into some molds as the fourth brother held them still.

After a long wait for the metal to cool, one of the men snapped open the mold and used his knife to pry out a brand-new coin. Freshly minted silver gleamed in the firelight.

Instead of sporting an eagle and the words "United States of America" like legitimate coinage, it was a simple disk, embossed with a name that would soon become famous across the Ozarks—Yocum.

The four Yocum brothers—Solomon, Jacob, Jess, and Mike—had settled on the James Fork of the White River valley deep in the rough hill country of the Ozarks, arriving in about 1818 and becoming one of the first white families to move there. Living in crude conditions far from any towns, they hunted, fished, and traded with local Indians for furs. There was little to distinguish them from any other frontiersmen until a decision in faraway Washington, DC, changed their fortunes forever.

The federal government decided to move the Delaware tribe into the James River region. The Delaware had originally come from the Delaware River area back east but had been steadily pushed out by rival tribes and white expansion. Having been in contact with whites for more than a century, they had taken on many of the white man's ways, including wearing European-style clothing and building log cabins. In other aspects of their culture, such as religion and the traditional hunt, they kept to the old ways.

Once the Delaware relocated, they quickly set up a string of villages along the upper James River and Kickapoo Prairie, each named after the local chief who ran it, such as Captain Pipe, Captain Beaver, Captain Patterson, and so on. The rank of "captain" was a term of honor for a local chief. These villages became the largest settlements in the Ozarks until Springfield started booming after the Civil War.

In compensation for losing their lands, the Delaware received $4,000 a year in silver coins, with the chiefs getting additional silver. Attracted by the money the Delaware had to spend, white merchants and craftsmen followed them to the area. The few whites who already lived nearby also jumped at the chance to earn some of the tribe's silver.

Not wanting to be left behind in the lucrative new Indian trade, Solomon Yocum moved onto Delaware Indian land along the James River sometime in the 1820s, where he traded alcohol for the silver the government gave them. Many writers have painted the Yocums as tricky double-dealers in their business with the Indians, but that isn't fair to the Yocums or the Delaware. The Yocums provided the Delaware with what they wanted, and the Delaware used their government stipend for what it was intended, to buy goods from the only merchants in the area.

The only problem was that selling alcohol to Indians was illegal.

The local federal Indian agent, John Campbell, wrote to his boss in St. Louis complaining, "Solomon Yoachum has erected a distillery . . . and has made a quantity of peach brandy and has been selling it for some time in quantities to the Indians. There is a number of those outlaw characters settled all below him who are also selling whiskey constantly to the Indians."

These illicit traders refused to pay rent for living on Indian land (probably because they traded booze in lieu of rent), and in July 1825 Campbell ordered Solomon Yocum off the reservation.

This made little difference to Solomon. He simply moved a little south of the Indian lands and opened up another distillery to produce whiskey and brandy. To cover their tracks, the Yocums melted down the US silver coins the Delaware paid them and recast them as their own "Yocum Dollars." They also acted as middlemen for other white traders, melting down their government coins and turning them into Yocum Dollars for a fee. The Yocums told outsiders that all their silver came from a rich "silver cave" they owned, but more likely the cave was just a secret location for their money-making business.

In 1829 the US government and the Delaware signed the James Fork Treaty, which made the tribe move to a new reservation in Kansas. The last of them left by 1831, but by then the Yocums had plenty of silver and Yocum Dollars had become the preferred currency over much of the region.

So the removal of the Delaware didn't matter much to the Yocums. They had already struck it rich. With the silver they bought land, mills, and huge cattle and swine herds. They became a leading family in the Ozarks, and when the famous travel writer Henry Rowe Schoolcraft passed through, Solomon Yocum served as his host and guide, showing him around the area and treating him to the local delicacy of roast beaver tail, also a favorite of Meriwether Lewis of Lewis and Clark fame.

Part of the success of the Yocum Dollar was that it fulfilled a critical need for reliable money on the frontier. While settlers tended to hunt, fish, or grow their own food, and made most everything else they required, they still needed money in some circumstances. Buying land from the government, for example, had to be done with cash, and traveling salesmen generally demanded money for any articles from civilization they brought along to peddle.

But money was always in short supply. In these early years the Missouri Legislature created two banks but both failed, and the government didn't try again until 1836. A branch of the national bank opened in St. Louis in 1829, but it too went out of business in 1833, a victim of recession and political infighting over whether the federal government should even have a bank. To make up for the lack of money, local organizations such as cities and counties often printed their own paper currency. People derisively called these notes "shinplasters" after small pieces of paper soaked in vinegar, tar, or tobacco juice and plastered over the leg to cure sores.

As the name suggests, shinplasters didn't gain the consumers' confidence. Printers, enchanted with the idea of printing their own money, usually printed too much and ended up lowering its value. Counterfeits were common, and one county's money often wouldn't be accepted in another county. If an organization stopped printing money, all their old money usually became worthless, and if a bank went out of business, its money lost all value as well. People trusted out-of-state money even less, because in those days of chaotic finances and slow communication, nobody could know for sure if a note issued from, say, a bank in Illinois would still be valid, or even if the bank existed.

With no gold or silver being mined in Missouri, the only sources of precious metal were government coins, always in short supply, and Spanish coins coming up from the Santa Fe Trail. Spanish coins were highly valued, but there were never enough to go around. People in the Ozarks could easily find the locally produced Yocum Dollars, and the Yocums were smart enough to make them of good quality. In fact, they contained more silver than US government silver coins.

This nearly got the Yocums into trouble. When a settler tried to buy some land from the government land office in Springfield with Yocum Dollars, the clerk said the coins were counterfeit. The settler got angry and said the money was good, being made of pure silver. The clerk sent one off to Washington to be tested and discovered the man had spoken the truth. The government purportedly sent an agent to find the fabled silver cave, but he got the runaround from the Yocums and returned to the nation's capital empty-handed.

The Yocums played on the old legends of the silver cave to cover their tracks. While minting coins wasn't illegal, trading booze to the Indians definitely was, so it made sense to hide the evidence by getting rid of the government coins and making up a story about a silver cave. Even today, descendants of the Yocums and many other locals tell the tale that the family got the silver cave in exchange for some blankets, soap, and two horses. A little thought will show why this isn't true. The Delaware were far too savvy by this time to give away a valuable silver mine for cheap goods they could easily buy after a bit of digging. Of course, a few individuals could have betrayed their tribe by telling the secret of the mine in order to get those horses, but certainly both they and the Yocums would have been killed by the rest of the tribe once it was discovered.

A different take on the tale explains away this problem by saying the Delaware only revealed the location of the silver cave once the government told them they would be relocated again. The problem with this story, of course, is that the Yocum Dollars started circulating well *before* the Delaware relocated, and the source dried up after the Delaware left.

Another problem arises with the geology of Missouri. Silver hardly exists in the state; nobody has ever discovered any major veins. The only silver mine that ever operated in Missouri, in Madison County, lasted less than three years, from 1877 to 1879. In later years production of silver in Missouri steadily rose, but this only became possible after the development of modern techniques that can separate trace amounts of silver from the state's abundant lead deposits. This process didn't exist in the early to mid nineteenth century.

Be that as it may, the story of how the Yocums got their hands on the silver cave is still a good one and worth retelling. A group of Indian braves supposedly took the Yocums to a narrow valley where a small hole led to a cave nearly filled with silver. One legend says there were two veins of pure silver, one thirty feet long and another twenty feet long. The Yocums, delighted with their purchase, hid it by building a cabin right in front of the entrance, fashioning a secret door in the cellar that led to the mine.

While the story of the silver mine is almost certainly fiction, the Yocums encouraged its belief. They would often leave on hunting trips for several days, hinting that they were heading off to the mine. Greedy locals would follow them, but the Yocums had an expert knowledge of the land and always managed to shake them. This cat-and-mouse game only added to their mystique.

The idea of a silver cave was already an old legend by the time the Yocums got to the Ozarks. Some of the earliest French settlers a century before had come to the region because they believed it to be rich in silver. They soon left disappointed, but the legend of a cave with an immensely rich vein of silver never died. The Yocums revived it so successfully, its story has endured to the present day.

Legend says the mine was finally lost when James Yocum and his Delaware wife, Winona, got killed in a cave-in either in 1846 or 1847, and the other Yocums decided it would be too dangerous to continue mining and left for the California gold rush. The truth is a bit more mundane. What actually happened was that the real source of the silver, the Delaware tribe, left the area. By this time the Yocums had already bought their giant herds of pigs and cattle, lived comfortably on large farms, and had built prosperous businesses such as gristmills. They'd put down roots in the area and saw little reason to leave to continue their illegal activities in the Delaware's new home.

Solomon Yocum did go to the gold rush, however, perhaps thinking that he could strike it rich in a real mine. He didn't, and died in 1850. Solomon's descendants left for the California gold rush in 1851.

Another legend says that as Solomon lay dying, he gasped out directions to the mine to his grandson William, who drew a crude map to the site. One of his descendants, Joseph Yocum, later used this map in a fruitless search for the mine in Taney County in 1958. What it took him a while to realize, though, was that the western portion of Taney County became Stone County the year after Solomon died. Joseph Yocum looked there too, but found nothing. His search wasn't helped by all the twentieth-century dam projects that had turned streams into lakes and completely changed the look of much of the area. All the little creeks and pioneer cabins on the map had long since disappeared.

The Yocum Dollar was long gone too. Its value and high demand proved to be its undoing. The silver content was so high, speculators melted it down for the precious metal. While the Yocum Dollars vanished, the legend of the mine never died. The May 7, 1923, issue of the *Springfield Daily Leader* reported that when workers tore up the floor of an old cabin by Indian Creek, they found a Yocum Dollar. While they had only been hired to replace the floor, they started tearing up the entire cabin looking for more coins. Their vandalism was rewarded with the discovery of four more Yocum Dollars. This news led to a flood of outsiders pouring into the region, shovels in hand, looking for the silver cave. All of them left disappointed, but it created a good business for local farmers, who acted as guides and cooks and sold homemade treasure maps.

The majority of hill folk had stopped believing in the legend of the silver cave by this time. After all, hadn't the last surviving brother who knew the secret of its location, Solomon Yocum, left the state? Why would he leave to risk everything in the gold rush if he had a perfectly good mine at home? And why didn't any of the Yocum clan still living in the region, and there were hundreds of them, know or find out the secret?

But not all locals have stopped believing. Artie Ayres, son of one of the lucky workmen who tore up the old cabin, remained convinced the silver cave story was true, and spent his entire life looking for it. While he searched in vain, he did write a book of local history and became a well-known guide to the area.

While most locals may not have believed the myth, that didn't stop them from telling the "furriners," usually gullible city slickers with more money than sense, that they knew "just about" where the mine was, and would be happy to show them the location . . . for a small fee, of course.

The legend got another shot in the arm in 1974 when a treasure hunter claimed to have found 236 Yocum Dollars in a sealed metal box buried near Branson, Missouri. While this led to another rush of articles and searches for the mine, the treasure hunter never showed any of the supposed Yocum Dollars to a museum or coin expert for examination, so they may have been forgeries, common enough in the antique coin trade, or they may simply have never existed.

In another strange twist to the tale, a different Yocum Dollar actually preceded the American dollar and gave it its name. The Yocums originally came from Germany, getting their name from one of that country's saints, Saint Joachim of Floris (ca. 1145–1202). In the sixteenth century a large silver mine in Bohemia was named after the saint and the mine started minting a coin called the "Joachimstaler," eventually shortened to "thaler." The Dutch later minted a coin called the "daler," which circulated in Dutch settlements such as New Amsterdam, later called New York City. When the United States became a nation, they took the name and anglicized it to "dollar."

One Yocum Dollar has gone up for sale to the public in modern times. In 1984 the coin catalog *World Exonumia* included a supposed example for sale alongside a photograph. It said "Yoachum" on one side with thirteen stars and the date 1822, and the other had written upon it "United States

The only known example of what might be a Yocum Dollar, sold by a coin dealer in the 1980s. It matches the description of the fabled coin, but it's impossible to prove it's an original and not an early reproduction. *Courtesy World Exonumia*

of America 1 Dollar." The piece was crude and worn and appeared to have been made on a hand-struck die. An analysis showed it had 92.49 percent silver plus or minus 2 percent. It's interesting that the coin dealers themselves wouldn't swear to its authenticity, but suggested it may be "a modern fantasy piece made in the 1920's or later." But one has to wonder, would a tourist gimmick have so much real silver in it?

A hundred and fifty years after their deaths, the Yocums are still eluding pursuit.

The Slicker War
Vigilantes and Vendettas
in the Early Ozarks

Screams cut through the night as the hickory switch slashed across the man's bare back. He was tied to a tree in front of his Ozark cabin, his crying wife and children held at bay by the barrel of a shotgun. A group of vigilantes stood around the tree where they had bound their victim, cheering and laughing as the strongest among them used all his muscle to whip the thin length of wood across bloody flesh. The man sagged against the tree, barely conscious as blood streamed down his legs and onto the ground.

"Get out of Benton County in ten days or we'll be back to finish the job!" one of his attackers warned.

Whooping with glee and firing their revolvers in the air, the group mounted up and rode off into the night, leaving the family to care for the battered victim as best they could.

They had just been visited by the Slickers.

It all started when the Turk family moved to Benton County in 1839 from Tennessee, settling on the Twenty-Five Mile Prairie just north of modern Quincy. At first the newcomers appeared to be prosperous, educated farmers, but what people didn't know was that Hiram and Martha Turk and their sons James, Tom, Nathan, and Robert had moved there to dodge thousands of dollars of debt and Hiram's charges of affray (brawling), trespassing, gambling, attempted murder, and murder. He'd managed to get free because of his connections with powerful people, but it had become distinctly uncomfortable for the Turk family in Tennessee.

The Turks dressed well, spoke well, and had money to spend, so they appeared to be an excellent addition to the community, but soon people learned otherwise. Hiram and his eldest boy, James, drank heavily, and as the whiskey flowed their tempers turned foul. Tom, the middle boy, stood an intimidating six feet six inches. Most of his three hundred pounds was muscle, the rest anger and bad attitude. Nathan and Robert were still in their teens, but followed in the footsteps of their father and older brothers. Together they made a frightening group.

True to their nature, the first thing they did was open a tavern where the rougher element in the area lounged around, gambling and guzzling whiskey.

Within months the Turks got into trouble with their neighbor John Graham when he paid a $20 debt to Hiram with a counterfeit note. Twenty dollars was a lot of money at the time, so Hiram flew into a rage when he discovered the trick.

Later that day Hiram's son James was riding along and saw Graham riding toward him. James dismounted and approached, wielding a club. Graham warned him off, but James grabbed the bridle of Graham's horse and whipped out his Bowie knife.

Narrowly avoiding the sharp blade as it slashed by, Graham leapt off his horse and ran away, James hot on his heels, swearing he'd kill him. Suddenly Graham spun around and pointed a pistol at James, telling him that if he took another step, he'd be a dead man.

But James had his blood up and kept on coming. Graham pulled the trigger, but instead of a loud bang, he only heard an ineffective click as the gun misfired. James smacked him to the ground with his club and struck him on the head with his knife. Just then a neighbor intervened and held James back long enough for Graham to stagger to his horse and gallop away. He returned minutes later, having retrieved another gun, and it became James's turn to run.

The next day the justice of the peace showed up at the Turk home with a posse and took James into custody. For some unknown reason they didn't disarm him and let Tom and Hiram come along. When they arrived at the Graham home to hold a hearing, James refused to enter, and Graham refused to come out until they disarmed James. The officers moved to take James's gun, but Tom Turk pulled out a pistol and told them to stay back. The Turks went home, but their troubles were far from over.

The entire affair ended up in the courts. Hiram accused Graham of passing counterfeit currency, but the fake $20 bill had disappeared and the charges came to nothing. Somehow all the charges against the Turks got dropped as well.

Only two months later, Hiram Turk broke into the home of another of his neighbors, Archibald Cock, and threatened to kill him for reasons that have since been forgotten. The court dropped these charges too. It's not clear why the Turks seemed immune to prosecution, but the family apparently had friends as well as enemies, and the local law seemed reluctant to take sides.

Worse came that summer.

Just to the northeast of the Turk place flowed the Pomme de Terre River. Andrew Jones and his large clan had lived there in simple cabins since the earliest days of settlement. They were crude, illiterate folk, more interested in gambling and horse racing than education. Many locals said Andrew was a horse thief, but they said this only in whispers, because the Jones clan was related by marriage to many of the prominent families in the county.

Considering his character, it's not surprising Andrew liked to loaf around the Turk tavern. On Election Day of 1840, a large crowd gathered to vote, drink, and watch horse races. Andrew Jones and James Turk bet on a race, but fell into dispute about who won. In typical Turk family style, James struck Andrew with a rock. People jumped in on both sides, and soon the election party became a swirling mass of shouting men and flying fists.

Three of the Turk brothers were fined $100 each for rioting, but Hiram used his mysterious connections to get a remit from the governor. The courts also charged Hiram and James with rioting but put off the case until the following year.

Hiram had something else to celebrate as well. On Election Day he got elected justice of the peace. Now he and his sons could drink, gamble, and fight with little fear of the consequences.

James Turk hated one of their neighbors, a man named Abraham Nowell who had been a member of the jury that indicted his father and brother for helping him escape the posse, and now Nowell planned to be a witness at their trial for the tavern riot. James swore he would "take the damned old son of a bitch off his horse and whip him, so he can't go to court."

On the day of the trial, Nowell and some friends rode through the countryside toward the courthouse. As they stopped at a stream to drink, James rode past. He taunted Nowell, hinting he would settle on his land, and the conversation grew so heated, James drew out his revolver and advanced on Nowell, who grabbed a pistol and told him to stop. When James kept coming, Nowell killed him with a single shot.

Fearing the Turk clan more than the law, Nowell fled the county, only sneaking back in April 1842 to stand trial. The court ruled he had fired in self-defense.

The Turks wanted blood. It was all right for them to go free after committing crimes, but when someone raised a hand against their family, they had to pay. Unfortunately for the residents of Benton and Polk Counties, lots of people would pay.

Many of the Turks' neighbors had tired of the family's arrogance and violence, and since the law obviously wasn't going to help, they decided to take matters into their own hands. Archibald Cock organized a small group, including Andrew Jones, to oppose the Turk clan and their allies. They signed a solemn oath to kill Hiram.

On July 17, 1841, they got their chance.

Hiram and his followers were riding along a road through a brushy hollow one day when a shot rang out from the bushes. Hiram toppled off his horse, shouting, "I am a dead man!" The shooter disappeared into the thick brush before anyone could identify him. Hiram's friends carried him to a nearby cabin and summoned a doctor, and the spirited man lingered between life and death for three weeks before breathing his last.

Everyone suspected Andrew Jones. The courts indicted him for murder, and several of his friends for conspiracy to commit murder, but found them all innocent for lack of evidence. Jones celebrated his victory by stealing a neighbor's bull, cooking it, and inviting his friends to a big feast. Now the Jones clan, not the Turk family, got its way in Benton County.

This was too much for the surviving Turk brothers. Tom Turk organized a group of about thirty men who swore to uphold the law against horse thieves, counterfeiters, and murderers. While this sounds a bit hypocritical considering how the Turks treated their neighbors, on the rough frontier people had more loyalty to their families and friends than they did to any abstract concept of law and order.

One of the new recruits was Isom Hobbs, an old friend of the Turk family from their Tennessee days. Like Hiram, he had been accused of murder back home and decided to move to Missouri. Many in the group had similar characters, but others were respectable folk in Polk County. These men probably took the group's oath at face value, thinking they had joined a vigilante group, but it was really a vendetta of one band of outlaws against another, a turf war over who got to terrorize the region.

The Turk faction had deeper motives than revenge. Most of the men were relative newcomers interested in opening up the region to commerce. They generally voted Democratic, disliked paper currency (much of which was counterfeit and all of which had dubious value), and came from educated families. They opposed older settlers like the Jones clan, who led a simpler life of hunting and fishing and had little use for "development." Turk and his allies were mostly based around Warsaw, the Benton County seat, while the older settlers concentrated to the south around Bolivar, the seat of Polk County.

On January 28, 1842, the Turks' new group claimed their first victims. Two men complained that while they had been racing horses with Andrew Jones and his friend Thomas

Meadows, some of their horses had been stolen. That's all the evidence Tom Turk and his crew needed. If the name Andrew Jones was in any way related to horse thievery, he must be guilty, him and his friend. Tom led his men on a fifteen-mile ride to Andrew's house, but only found his brother and another man. They threatened them with a whipping and ordered them to leave the county, and then proceeded to the home of Thomas Meadows. Tying Meadows to a tree, they stripped the bark off of some hickory switches and whipped him until his back was crisscrossed with bloody stripes. Witnesses claim that his blood created a gory stream that flowed a full six feet away.

Taking the bark off a switch was called "slicking" in local parlance, so Tom Turk's vigilantes became known as "Slickers" after their favorite method of punishment. That same day the Slickers went to the home of William Brookshire, a friend of Jones and Meadows, and gave him the same treatment.

"Slicking," whipping with branches stripped of their bark, was a common and painful punishment on the frontier. *Used by permission, State Historical Society of Missouri, Columbia*

As the hickory switches slashed into his back, Meadows admitted that Andrew Jones had stolen those horses. Brookshire named Jones and two other men as the murderers of Hiram Turk. Of course, being whipped is liable to make someone say anything he thinks his torturers want to hear, but these tales were proof enough for the Slickers.

Over the next few days, the vigilantes slicked three more friends of their enemies. In one case Robert, the youngest of the Turk brothers at only seventeen, gave the first few licks before letting a more experienced hand take over.

The Slickers didn't just whip people to punish them and to extract information; they also used the raids to scare families off their land so the Slickers could buy it. The terrorized families usually sold at any price so they could get out of the county as quickly as possible.

By this time the more law-abiding members of the community had had enough. On March 21 the militia set out to capture Andrew Jones, which they did after he tried to shoot one of the militiamen who also happened to be a Slicker. Jones's gun misfired, which was good for him because the court only charged him with attempted murder and let him out on bond. The sight of large numbers of armed, trained militiamen marching along the country roads helped calm the situation for a time.

Like before, when guns didn't work the two sides tried to get their revenge through the courts, filing countless charges and countercharges. The streets of Warsaw filled with large bands of armed Slickers and their enemies, while the militia cast a nervous eye on both. Several fights ensued, and in one incident a group of anti-Slickers threatened to storm a building where the Slickers had gathered, and the Slickers scared them off by sticking a stovepipe out the window and announcing they had a cannon.

As usual, people were either found not guilty or simply skipped town. Andrew Jones decided not to risk trial and fled. While this got rid of the Turk family's main rival, it couldn't have been very satisfactory to them.

On October 18 Abraham Nowell, an old rival of the Turk family from the very start of the troubles, walked out the front door of his cabin and bent over a barrel to get a bucket of water. Just then a shot rang out from the bushes. Nowell stood up in surprise, and another bullet tore through his chest. His wife rushed to his side, screaming for help. She saw two shadowy figures slip away through the brush but couldn't identify them.

The killers soon identified themselves. Within hours of the shooting, Isom Hobbs bragged that he'd "bagged a deer" and hinted that Tom Turk was a coward. Apparently Tom had taken the first shot, and Isom thought he'd missed on purpose to avoid responsibility for the murder.

Soon both sides took to erecting fake graves by the side of the road bearing the names of their enemies. A Baptist minister gave a sermon against the Slickers, and one loudmouthed Slicker swore all Baptists would be run out of the area. This united the more peaceful citizens against the Slickers.

One night three shots rang out near the cabin of William Metcalf, a neighbor of the Turks who had become one of their many enemies. One bullet cracked through the door and hit Jacob Dobkins, Abraham Nowell's son-in-law. Dobkins lingered between life and death for two days. A judge claimed he heard the young man say Hobbs and the Turks shot him, and so he called out the militia, led by Major Nathan Rains, to arrest every man in the Hobbs and Turk families. A bunch of anti-Slickers from Benton County, as well as a group of angry Baptists, came along too. They rounded up Nathan Turk and surrounded a cabin where Isom Hobbs and several other Slickers were hiding out. The militia told them they had the place surrounded and would set it on fire, and the Slickers soon surrendered.

Once again the wheels of frontier justice turned, and creaked to a stop. Prosecutors had no real evidence against the Slickers and eventually released them, but not before the Turks filed suit against Rains for false arrest. The Slickers turned out to have a better case than their enemies and got Rains court-martialed for misconduct of office.

Despite several brushes with the law, Isom Hobbs didn't keep his mouth shut. He kept bragging about killing someone and took to calling his rifle "Old Abram." He boasted it was accurate to ninety-six yards, the distance from which Abraham Nowell had been shot.

At harvest time in 1844, Isom Hobbs and Tom Turk were working in the same field. It must have been a tense situation, because Hobbs still felt Tom had been cowardly during the shooting of Nowell, and Tom would have heard of those accusations. Soon tempers flared. The two men faced off with scythes, but a deadly duel was averted when Tom fled the field.

Humiliated and afraid for his life, Tom announced he would leave the county. But it was not to be. On August 9, as Tom rode home from a blacksmith shop, Isom Hobbs hid in the brush, waiting for him. One shot from "Old Abram," and

Tom pitched from the saddle. Neighbors carried his body to a nearby home, and Isom showed up to "pay his respects," rubbing the victim's head and saying, "You have been a brave fellow, Tom, but they got you at last."

"They" might have gotten Tom, but his younger brother Robert still lived. A few weeks later he hid beside a road outside Warsaw where he knew the Hobbs family would ride. Robert created a blind out of brush, like he was going to hunt deer, and set in for a long wait. When the Hobbs family came into view, he was frustrated to see Isom wasn't among them. Shrugging his shoulders, he aimed at Isom's brother Jeff and took him out with a single bullet. It wasn't the revenge he wanted, but it was a start.

A posse grabbed Robert a couple of days later, but once again the courts couldn't gather enough evidence to convict and he walked free. Authorities captured Isom Hobbs soon after, but he somehow managed to get the key to his cell. After he escaped, he hid the key in a tree stump and wrote a letter to the sheriff telling him where he could find it. He wouldn't enjoy his freedom long, however. After fleeing to Mississippi, he got into more trouble with the law, and a posse gunned him down.

Andrew Jones came to a bad end too. In 1844 he and some accomplices savagely murdered and robbed three Indians in Texas, one of them a young boy. Two Indians who escaped identified the killers, and Andrew Jones ended his long career in crime at the end of a rope. Nathan Turk died shortly thereafter in Shreveport, Louisiana, knifed during an argument over a card game. Robert, the last surviving Turk brother, took his mother, Martha, to Kentucky to start a new life.

It had been seven long, brutal years. Benton and Polk Counties were nearly bankrupted from the costs of conducting so many trials, but the troubles finally subsided. Most criminals had been killed or run out of the area, and those who remained feared another cycle of vendettas and kept quiet. Peace had finally returned to the rugged Ozarks.

William Quantrill
Terror of Civil War Missouri

The morning of August 21, 1863, dawned clear and warm. The residents of Lawrence, Kansas, woke from their sleep and started going about their daily rounds. Men and boys did chores while their wives or mothers prepared breakfast. The town lay quiet, and the Civil War seemed far away. If a few noticed the rising column of dust to the east, they probably thought it was some merchant wagons coming to trade, or a column of federal troops passing through.

Actually, that column of dust was being kicked up by some four hundred raiders from Missouri, rebel "bushwhackers" led by the greatest guerrilla chieftain of them all, William Clarke Quantrill.

The bushwhackers had always dreamed of hitting Lawrence. For years it had been the center for the state's abolitionist movement and was the home of Senator James Lane, one of the state's most prominent "Jayhawkers," antislavery guerrillas almost as brutal as the bushwhackers. But the town lay forty miles west of the heavily patrolled state line. That Quantrill and his men made it there undetected is a tribute to their skill at hit-and-run warfare.

For days the Missourians had ridden west, dodging Union patrols and burning with hatred. Shortly before, a building in Kansas City used as a prison for many of the guerrillas' female relatives had collapsed, and some had died. William Anderson, one of Quantrill's lieutenants, lost a sister in the accident. A rumor spread that Union soldiers had undermined the building on purpose, and from then on Anderson rode into battle muttering his sister's name, killing everyone he could while foaming at the mouth. He became known as "Bloody Bill."

Despite its obvious potential as a target, there were no trained soldiers in town on the day of the attack. All of them were away, ironically enough, hunting bushwhackers.

The guerrilla horde thundered toward town. Just to the east of Lawrence lived the Reverend S. S. Snyder, a United Brethren Church minister and recruiter for the Second Colored Kansas Volunteers. He sat outside milking a cow when the little army galloped past. Two of the guerrillas rode into his yard and shot him dead.

Soon they poured into town, breaking into separate groups and riding up all the streets. As people poked their heads out windows, they saw men everywhere. Confusion reigned. Many of the guerrillas wore captured federal uniforms, a favorite disguise, but as the air filled with gunshots and screams, it became clear this was no Union army.

A large group headed toward the camps of the Fourteenth Kansas Regiment and Second Colored Regiment, both of which were made up of raw recruits who had not yet been issued guns. The bushwhackers slaughtered more than a dozen of them as the rest fled in panic.

Quantrill, a pistol in his hand, stood up in his stirrups and screamed to his men, "Kill! Kill and you will make no mistake. Lawrence should be thoroughly cleansed, and the only way to cleanse it is to kill! Kill!"

Quantrill's burning of Lawrence, Kansas, and the massacre of its male population was the worst civilian atrocity of the war and shocked the public in both the North and the South. *Courtesy Library of Congress*

Quantrill led a group to the Eldridge House hotel, the finest in town, and hustled the guests outside. The guerillas robbed the men, and if any gave the least sign of resistance, they gunned them down. Then they set fire to the building.

It wasn't the only place to burn. Quantrill had assembled a list of known Unionists. Detachments of guerrillas sought out their homes and shot the men in front of their families before torching the place.

All around town flames leapt into the air as more and more houses became engulfed. Dead bodies lay in the streets, boys as young as twelve beside men in their sixties, while bushwhackers looted homes and stores or drank themselves nearly unconscious.

Strangely, no women were seriously harmed. Quantrill had given strict orders about this. In the nineteenth century, chivalry still reigned, at least most of the time. "Bloody Bill" Anderson and some of the other guerrillas would, as the war dragged on and became ever more savage, soon count women among their lengthening list of victims.

But not in Lawrence. In fact, many Kansas women stood up to the guerrillas, dousing the flames as soon as Quantrill's men lit them, or hiding their menfolk and refusing to reveal their whereabouts.

As pandemonium spread, some citizens gathered rifles and hid in brick houses, fortifying the windows and doors with piles of furniture and firewood and sniping at any guerrilla who dared approach. Looking for easier prey, the bushwhackers hurried off to other parts of town.

One guerrilla, a Baptist preacher named Larkin Skaggs, tore down an American flag and tied it to a rope attached to his saddle. Then he rode up and down the street, dragging the flag behind him in the dirt.

After getting bored with this, Skaggs went after Judge Samuel Riggs, near the top of Quantrill's list. In 1860 Riggs had indicted Quantrill for several offenses, for which he was probably guilty. When Skaggs found Riggs and pointed his pistol at him, Riggs knocked it to one side and took off running. Skaggs urged his horse after the judge, but Riggs's wife grabbed onto Skaggs's bridle. Skaggs rode around, trailing the woman on the ground like the American flag and beating at her with his pistol, but she refused to let go until her husband got away.

Soon most names on Quantrill's list had been checked off, except for the name on top. The Jayhawk leader Jim Lane had fled into the countryside wearing only his nightshirt. Quantrill himself showed up at his home to kill him, but found only his wife. He cavalierly allowed Mrs. Lane to retrieve some of the family possessions before setting fire to the house, saying, "Give Mr. Lane my compliments. Please say I would be glad to meet him."

Mrs. Lane was not impressed and replied, "Mr. Lane would be glad to meet you under . . . more favorable circumstances."

Lane was no coward; he was gone only long enough to get a horse, a gun, and a few men before riding back into town, perhaps hoping for more favorable circumstances.

It was too late. The guerrillas had already left.

Just after nine in the morning, lookouts warned Quantrill that the federal cavalry was on its way, and he ordered his lieutenant William Gregg to round everyone up and head back to Missouri. Despite some being so drunk they could barely make it into their saddles, Gregg gathered all of them . . . save one.

Skaggs still rode around town, too drunk to notice everyone else had left. He occasionally stopped to take potshots at fleeing civilians or to steal something, but it took a while for the fact that he was alone to penetrate his bleary brain. When he finally figured it out he galloped off in panic, and straight into a posse of Kansans riding in the other direction. They disarmed him, and it wasn't long until a local boy named Billy Speer shot him. A Delaware Indian named White Turkey pegged him with an arrow and scalped him. Townspeople hanged his body from a tree and peppered it with bullets.

It was a hollow vengeance. About two hundred corpses littered the street, and much of the town lay in smoking ruins.

More vengeance was coming. Soon a sizable force of federal soldiers (this time with weapons), angry locals, and farmers from the surrounding area caught up with Quantrill's band and gave it a running fight all the way back into Missouri. At least forty guerrillas died in the pursuit.

Still the Unionists weren't satisfied. Lawrence was the worst atrocity against civilians in the war. General Thomas Ewing, commander of the District of the Border, issued General Order Number 11 to stamp out guerrilla activity in the region once and for all. It ordered all civilians living in Jackson, Cass, and Bates Counties, and part of Vernon County, to vacate their homes. If they could prove their loyalty, they could live near one of the military bases; everyone else had to leave the area. His men enforced the order with ruthless efficiency, burning homes and looting property on the least excuse, or no excuse at all. Tens of thousands of men, women, and children became impoverished refugees overnight, and the area was known as "The Burnt District" for years afterward. The savage raid on Lawrence led to an equally savage reprisal.

Nothing in Quantrill's childhood hinted that he would become the Civil War's most notorious guerrilla. Friends remembered him as quiet and intelligent, but an avid hunter and a good shot. He was born in Ohio in 1837, the eldest child of Thomas Quantrill, a tinker and school principal who often beat his son in public for no apparent reason. His father also got into several scrapes with neighbors and embezzled school funds. At sixteen William followed in his father's footsteps and became a schoolteacher. That same year his father died, and it is doubtful William shed many tears over his grave.

William soon set out to make his fortune, settling in Kansas in 1857 at a time when the territory was the center of the debate over the expansion of slavery, with proslavery bushwhackers and abolitionist Jayhawkers fighting for control. Quantrill worked on a farm for a while and the following year signed on as a teamster for the US Army during its expedition to suppress the Mormon rebellion in Utah. The experience began to change him. The teamsters were a rough lot, inclined to gamble, drink, and fight, and Quantrill gained a reputation as an avid gambler and a quick draw.

The following year he set out with eighteen associates to Colorado in search of gold, but the party ran out of food in the Rockies, suffered attacks by Indians, and got caught in a blizzard. Only he and six others survived. Like virtually everyone else who went to the Colorado gold rush, Quantrill didn't strike it rich. He was soon back in Kansas working as a teacher.

Quantrill had transformed from a quiet schoolboy to a tough young man. By 1860 the struggle between bushwhackers and Jayhawkers on the Missouri-Kansas border had become worse, much of the fighting simply masking outright banditry. Quantrill saw an opportunity for easy money. He stopped writing to his family and friends in Ohio, something he had continually done in all the years he'd been away. He simply left his old life behind.

Quantrill and his friends made money by kidnapping free blacks in Kansas and selling them as slaves in Missouri, or stealing slaves in Missouri and ransoming them back to their owners. They also stole horses and cattle, and while they claimed to be proslavery bushwhackers, they didn't mind stealing from proslavery men too.

Once the American Civil War started in April 1861, Quantrill saw a grand opportunity for more raiding. But he would now have to formally pick a side, and he picked the South.

Quantrill joined the Missouri Confederate army of General Sterling Price, seeing action at the battles of Wilson's Creek and Lexington before leaving during the Confederate retreat to Neosho. He returned to the Blue Springs area of Jackson County and soon gathered a group of bushwhackers. His education and intelligence, not to mention his ability with guns and horses, made him the obvious leader. Starting with only about a dozen men, Quantrill's band grew as he became more and more successful at robbing Union farmers and ambushing federal patrols and supply wagons.

By early 1862 he had become one of the most successful guerrillas in Missouri. When the Union army declared that guerrillas would be treated as bandits and not soldiers and would be executed rather than imprisoned, Quantrill and his men became even more determined. For the most part they stopped taking prisoners. What had started as a government tactic to reduce guerrilla action by striking fear into their hearts only made the war more savage.

Riding the best horses they could steal, and carrying rifles as well as several revolvers each, the guerrillas could outrun and outfight Union troops, who only carried single-shot muskets and rode government nags of indifferent quality. Since many Union troops in Missouri came from as far away as Iowa or even Colorado, and the guerrillas were generally local boys, the rebels knew the terrain better. They knew which farmers they could trust and where to find isolated campgrounds deep in the brush. Still, Quantrill and his men found themselves in many tight spots, sometimes getting surrounded as they rested at what they thought was a safe house and having to fight their way out.

Despite all this activity, Quantrill managed to find time to get a girlfriend, Sarah "Kate" King, an attractive farm girl who he introduced as his wife although there is no definitive proof they ever married. Kate claimed she was only thirteen when she fell in love with the guerrilla. Back in the nineteenth century people married a lot younger, but even so, Kate felt obligated to say in a later interview that she "looked sixteen."

As time went on, Quantrill and his men acted less like Confederate guerrillas and more like bandits. They robbed stagecoaches and civilians, accumulating vast amounts of loot while only occasionally remembering to attack Union troops. Not even Southern sympathizers felt safe from them. The raid on Lawrence was only the culmination of long months of lawlessness.

When autumn stripped the leaves from the bushes that hid their campgrounds, the guerrillas would head to Texas for the winter to loaf around, get drunk, spend and gamble their stolen money, and cause trouble. Confederate officials became increasingly annoyed. Numerous complaints from locals about getting robbed by the guerrillas made the local Confederate commander, Brigadier General Henry McCulloch, first try to reason with the guerrillas, then try to get them to join the regular army, and finally try to kick them out of the region. Nothing worked. Eventually he arrested Quantrill, but the guerrilla escaped.

At the same time, Quantrill was having increasing difficulty controlling his own men. Some of his lieutenants, such as "Bloody Bill" Anderson and William Gregg, split away from the group to head up their own commands. In the summer of 1864, another of his men, George Todd, overthrew him. Todd had nursed a longstanding grudge against Quantrill for not giving him more authority, and finally his patience broke. The two were playing cards one night when Quantrill accused him of cheating. Todd whipped out a pistol and told him to leave camp. Quantrill had no choice but to obey. Only a few men followed him.

Not even Quantrill could satisfy the fractious bushwhackers for long. Some of his men, like William Gregg, were appalled by the massacre at Lawrence and the increasing lack of discipline. Others, like Anderson and Todd, simply wanted more power for themselves.

Leading about twenty men, Quantrill returned to Missouri. He did a bit of raiding and helped out during General Price's final invasion of the state in late 1864, but when that invasion failed, he took it as a signal that the Confederate cause was lost. He and a few men headed to Kentucky, slipping across the heavily guarded Mississippi River in the dead of night. A surviving member of Quantrill's band claimed they planned to ride all the way to Washington and assassinate Abraham Lincoln. It is doubtful even Quantrill would be so bold. More likely he simply wanted to get away from the West, where he was known to everyone and hated by almost as many.

Like Missouri, Kentucky was full of bushwhackers, and the Union commander for the state, General John Palmer, swore to stamp them out. He started a "Secret Service" to track down all guerrillas, made up of men as lawless and deadly as the guerrillas themselves. He assigned one of them, a thief and murderer named Edwin Terrell, the task of hunting down Quantrill.

Quantrill acted cautiously in Kentucky. He and his men wore federal uniforms and passed themselves off as a Union patrol, one of their favorite tricks. Needing fresh mounts, they rode into Harrodsburg on January 29, 1865, to "requisition" some horses. The citizens grumbled, but everyone believed the men to be actual soldiers. It wasn't until a real Union officer objected to having his horse taken that their cover was blown.

"I have been a soldier for two years and you shall not take my horse," the officer complained when he saw a guerrilla sitting atop his prized gray mare.

When the man made no move to dismount, the officer added, "If this horse leaves this stable, it will be over my dead body."

The guerrilla whipped out his pistol, said, "That is a damned easy job," and shot the officer in the face.

Quantrill's men galloped out of town, swept through nearby Danville to steal more horses, and split up. Union cavalry set out in hot pursuit, discovered where one group of a dozen guerrillas had hidden in a house for the night, and killed four before the rest surrendered.

In the following days Quantrill became melancholy and desperate and talked increasingly of death. He continued to do his duty as a guerrilla, however, cutting telegraph lines and attacking a Union wagon train. While this helped the war effort, it also revealed his location.

On May 10 Terrell finally caught up with Quantrill at the farmhouse of a Southern sympathizer. Quantrill and twenty-one men were resting when their lookout saw a long line of riders carrying rifles crest the ridge in front of the barn. As usual, Quantrill and his men vaulted into their saddles, prepared to make one of their famous breakouts. Banging away with their pistols, they galloped away from the farm.

Quantrill, however, was not among them. His horse was a new "acquisition" and it hadn't gotten used to gunfire yet. It panicked and Quantrill couldn't get into the saddle. He ran down the path, calling for two of his men to wait for him, but before he could reach them a bullet hit him in the back, breaking his spinal cord and paralyzing him. He fell face first into the mud.

Quantrill struggled for life for almost a month. He received numerous visitors, including a Catholic priest who converted him, and several ladies. He gave instructions that his stolen loot be given to Kate, although apparently she never received it. He finally passed away on June 6, never having sent a message to the family he had turned his back on.

The butcher of Lawrence was dead.

The Other Harry Truman
Union Turncoat

Like the rest of Missouri during the Civil War, the north-central part of the state was at war with itself. Supporters of the Union and the Confederacy lived side by side. Rebel guerrillas, such as local boy Clifton Holtzclaw, hid in the thick woods and raided Unionists while federal troops, tipped off by loyal citizens, robbed and harassed secessionist civilians in an attempt to intimidate them into not supporting the guerrillas.

Into this maelstrom on June 5, 1864, rode a group of about twenty armed men. They looked tough, but what really worried the civilians was the fact that they didn't wear uniforms. Nobody knew which side they were on. Local Unionists grew suspicious, because rebel guerrillas often didn't wear uniforms, but on the other hand they sometimes liked to dress in captured federal uniforms to fool their enemies. Secessionists didn't know what to make of them. The riders eventually revealed that they were sent by the Union army. Loyal citizens breathed a sigh of relief while secessionists became worried, realizing they would be singled out for harsh treatment.

Both sides were wrong.

At the head of the column rode Jacob Terman, who often used the alias "Harry Truman" but was certainly *not* related to the more famous Missourian who would later bear that name. Terman/Truman had been sent by Major General William S. Rosecrans, Commander of the Department of

In Civil War Missouri, civilians often faced bands of armed men who wore no uniforms, or the uniforms of the opposite side. Pretending to be of the wrong allegiance could prove to be a fatal mistake. *Used by permission, State Historical Society of Missouri, Columbia*

Missouri, to hunt down Holtzclaw. The local guerrilla had recently terrorized the town of Keytesville in Chariton County. Holtzclaw's father had died at the hands of Union troops, and the guerrilla exacted a bloody vengeance, robbing and killing loyalist civilians. Truman was supposed to stop Holtzclaw's raids, which terrified Union men and embarrassed local Union commanders who seemed helpless to stop them, but Truman had other priorities.

The evening Truman's group rode into the area, a local Union man named Ephraim Clarke showed him the way to Holtzclaw's camp. Peering through the bushes at the large numbers of tough guerrillas eating their dinner and cleaning their guns by the campfire, Truman realized his small force would be no match for the heavily armed fighters. He and his men decided to ride to the nearby town of Bucklin for reinforcements. On the way they started robbing houses, not caring if they were owned by Unionist or rebel. As they stole a mare from a local minister, the man pleaded that it wasn't even his, but borrowed from a neighbor, and begged Truman not to take it. The renegade Union soldier laughed and said he would "take her if she belonged to Jesus Christ."

The minister also lost a sidesaddle and a riding skirt, which were taken for one of the two ladies who stood outside his house during the robbery. It is unclear who these women were, but Truman was known to travel with someone one local Union commander referred to as a "common, abandoned woman."

The following morning Truman and his men decided not to get the reinforcements or return to fight Holtzclaw. Looting civilians had turned out to be far more profitable, not to mention safer. Horses were the most valuable portable item, and they could always say they intended to deny supplies to the rebel guerrillas, who did their own share of horse thieving. Truman's band did show their Unionist sympathies when they came upon John Walker, a local secessionist who thought he faced rebel guerrillas. He told the attentive soldiers the names of several local Unionists and encouraged the group to attack them. This informing of neighbor against neighbor was all too typical of the Civil War in Missouri, but this time it backfired. Truman listened for a time, and then calmly ordered Walker hanged.

That night Truman finally did go get reinforcements at Bucklin, joining up with a detachment of the Ninth Missouri State Militia Cavalry commanded by Lieutenant Samuel Patterson. Since Truman had delayed so long, Holtzclaw had moved camp, so the search had to resume all over again. Truman, reeling in his saddle from a day of heavy drinking, didn't seem in much of a hurry. The group stayed the night at the house of a local civilian, and the next morning Truman relieved him of a horse and two guns. They then went to the camp where Truman had spied on Holtzclaw previously, but the guerrillas were long gone. Lieutenant Patterson, disgusted with Truman's behavior, took his men and rode off.

Word of Truman's conduct had made its way up the army chain of command, and General Fisk, who had enough troubles with secessionists in his district without Truman stirring them up, sent a telegraph to General Rosecrans complaining of Truman's behavior and asking that he be removed. Fisk wrote that Truman was "guilty of all the crimes that I . . . am under obligation to put down." Rosecrans told Fisk to do what he wanted with Truman.

Truman was blissfully unaware of this, busy as he was having fun at the local citizenry's expense. He and his men thundered into Keytesville, announcing they were guerrillas. Some of them rode into the local grocery store and demanded whiskey. The band rounded up all the civilians and Truman treated them to a long, angry speech, saying he intended to loot every Southern man in the area. To prove his point, Truman rode to the home of a man who bragged about being a bushwhacker, hauled him back to Keytesville, and hanged him from a tree in front of the hotel. His men also shot dead another Southern sympathizer. They then proceeded to drink themselves into a stupor, stealing whatever took their fancy.

The next day they grew even meaner, killing three locals, including a sixteen-year-old boy reputed to be one of

Holtzclaw's guerrillas. On June 11 Truman moved his men out of Chariton County, triumphantly leading a string of forty stolen horses and seventy-five black men whom he intended to force into the Union army.

While the rebel bushwhackers were notorious for looting and killing, Jacob Terman/Harry Truman, a Unionist in the employ of the federal government, had proven he could loot and kill with the best of them.

Despite his brief notoriety, very little is actually known about the real life of Jacob Terman. Though he gave an account of his past, he can hardly be considered a reliable source. He said he was born in Ohio in 1829 and served with the Texas Rangers during the war with Mexico before ending up in Kansas in the 1850s, where he took part in the border war that trained so many of Missouri's most notorious outlaws. Terman joined the abolitionist Jayhawkers, but apparently his main motivation for this was because proslavery bushwhackers had destroyed some of his property.

Always an opportunist, Truman saw the Civil War as a great way to make money. He knew the border district and its people well and could provide valuable services to the federal troops as a scout and spy. He acted like a chameleon, pretending he was a bushwhacker to infiltrate their bands. Truman often boasted that he had infiltrated the outfits of famous rebel guerrillas such as William Clarke Quantrill and George Todd, and to prove he was a "real" bushwhacker, shared in the fighting and pillaging along with his new compatriots.

Despite his dubious character, the Union command kept him on because he provided vital intelligence. Much of the populace hated the Federals, and even many loyal civilians were too afraid of the bushwhackers to give the troops any information, so the officers took whatever help they could and didn't get too picky about the source.

Truman was a master at getting what he wanted and could seemingly fast-talk his way out of any tight spot. He wrote his initials, birthday, and a Freemason symbol on his arm to identify himself to Union officials. Membership in the Freemasons could get a man out of a lot of trouble in those days, because even if two Masons fought on opposite sides of the war, they would usually not kill one another knowingly. Truman also infiltrated the Confederate secret society of the Knights of the Golden Circle, or at least knew enough about it that he could pass himself off as a member, and this once saved him from a Confederate firing squad.

In 1863 his tricks almost caught up with him while working undercover in George Todd's guerrilla band. He got a bit overeager looting loyalist civilians, and the Union command had him arrested and clapped in jail. He got out, though, because the Union army needed information on the Knights of the Golden Circle that only Truman could supply. The Knights were a secret society that acted to undermine Union efforts throughout the border states. Federal commanders saw them as a grave threat. Their real power is debated by historians, but Truman played on Unionist fears and gave the government a detailed account of the secret society's activities. Whether this information was true or not is another matter. He received orders to accompany a force of soldiers to round up members of the Knights, and his word sent more than a dozen men to jail.

Summer of that year saw him working in southeast Missouri, claiming to have infiltrated the army of Confederate Brigadier

General M. Jeff Thompson, nicknamed the "Swamp Fox" for his practice of hiding out in the region's almost impassable swamps. Whether Truman ever did infiltrate the rebel army is questionable, but his intelligence sounded plausible enough that he was kept on in Union employ.

Union command transferred Truman to central Missouri, which had the worst amount of bushwhacker activity of any part of the state at the time. Union soldiers weren't safe outside their own blockhouses, and attacks on transport wagons and mail couriers had gotten so bad that Union troops started forcing known secessionists to do these duties, figuring the bushwhackers wouldn't kill them. Even if they did, no Union officer would count it as much of a loss.

Truman didn't make a good impression at his new job, showing up drunk for his first meeting with his new commander, Colonel John Sanderson. Despite this, he got permission to head north and meet Brigadier General Clinton Fisk, commander of the District of North Missouri, which was similarly plagued with bushwhackers. Fisk wasn't impressed with Truman either, but orders were orders and the general let him continue with the mission.

Truman rode to Macon, in Macon County, and demanded weapons, supplies, and men from the local garrison of the Ninth Missouri State Militia Cavalry. He told the militiamen that he was a United States detective and Captain of Scouts. He was neither of these things, but it sounded good and he presented himself with such authority that the soldiers believed him. They gave him all the equipment he needed plus twenty men familiar with the area, and he proceeded to ride around the region looking for rebels. They didn't wear uniforms so they could pass themselves off as bushwhackers in order to convince local secessionists into revealing themselves. These trusting souls were then robbed and arrested. The tactic proved both profitable and effective.

Complaints poured into General Fisk's headquarters, and Fisk wrote to the central command that Truman "was bringing upon me more trouble than all the bushwhackers of North Missouri combined." Fisk recalled him, but Truman went over his head to General Rosecrans, the man who had sent him out in the first place. Rosecrans ordered him to continue his hunt for rebels, and this, combined with copious and almost constant drinking, gave him the courage to make his rampage through the region, killing, burning, and looting, while doing virtually nothing to hunt down Holtzclaw.

But Truman had gone a step too far. He had killed too many people, robbed too much. The papers railed against him, even the Unionist ones. Faced with mounting pressure and dubious results, the Union command decided to put him on trial.

Truman was put into the jailhouse at St. Joseph, and the stolen goods were sent back to Macon. If the victims could prove ownership and their loyalty to the Union, they could have their property back. This last stipulation is significant, because many of those robbed were known to have sympathies for the South. While the government planned to punish Truman for his crimes, they didn't mind profiting from them. The black men were offered positions in the Union army, but most returned to their homes. They had heard about the low and infrequent pay for black regiments, and their first impression of a Union officer couldn't have been a good one.

Back in Chariton County, Truman's depredations encouraged the bushwhackers to retaliate, killing eight Unionists and causing a mass exodus of civilians from the region. Instead of putting down guerrilla activity, Truman had only encouraged it.

Truman's trial in July and August became the sensation of the season. The papers devoted large amounts of space to the testimony, and the editorials were predominantly negative against him. All but the most rabid Unionists could see that Truman's actions had only made the situation worse, although a few ardently Unionist editors claimed he was a noble officer acting on the highest principles to defend the country.

The prosecution brought several witnesses to the stand, including Ephraim Clarke, who had been hired to guide Truman's group of renegades through the local area, and a doctor who witnessed one of the hangings. All of them stated that those who had been hanged had "good reputations," indicating they were probably not secessionists. None asserted that the victims had been guerrillas or troublemakers. Truman cross-examined the witnesses, but made little headway. When he asked about the loyalty of one witness, the prosecution objected and the judge sustained the objection. Truman's witch-hunting tactics weren't going to work in the courtroom.

He did, however, put up a surprisingly good defense for himself, and the court transcripts show his quick intelligence. He managed to cast doubt over some of the testimony and distance himself from the depredations done by his men while not in his presence. The widow of one victim even testified that Truman told her he hadn't ordered her husband's killing, and that his men had exceeded their orders. Truman also managed to cast doubt on the testimony of Ephraim Clarke. Truman had cleverly gotten Clarke to do much of the dirty work, and kept others from hearing him give Clarke orders. Clarke acted sanctimonious in court, but Truman made it look like Clarke was responsible for at least some of the crimes. In Clarke's case it appears both sides told the truth; the man was an opportunist who didn't mind taking pay for snitching on his neighbors (pay that, he complained to the court, he had never received) but became righteously indignant about Truman's methods once the officer faced a murder charge.

Despite Truman's able defense, the judge and jury clearly saw that he carried the ultimate responsibility for most, if not all, of the crimes. They found him guilty of murder and theft and sentenced him to hang, but General Rosecrans, perhaps feeling guilty for his own involvement in the affair, commuted the sentence to hard labor. It wasn't the first or the last time a corrupt Union officer got away with murder in Missouri.

Even behind bars Truman could be dangerous to his enemies. Those civilians who had dared testify against him had their houses burned; many turned up dead. Apparently Truman had friends outside of prison who were just as vicious as he was.

Despite this, General Rosecrans tried to help him. He forwarded Truman's military record to higher channels. As the military bureaucracy waffled, Truman was twice set free on parole and twice had that parole revoked, but eventually Rosecrans's support made enough of an impression that the charges were dropped entirely and Truman became a free man in April 1865.

The war was winding down. General Robert E. Lee's Army of Northern Virginia, the pride of the Confederacy, had surrendered the same month Truman walked out of jail for the last time, and other rebel armies would soon follow suit. The guerrillas, however, hesitated to give themselves up. They had been branded as criminals during the war and didn't trust the government's offers of amnesty.

Truman soon returned to Missouri, claiming he could get some of the guerrilla bands to surrender. After being given men and equipment, he roved across the northern part of the state, drinking and stealing. Once again Union officials sent him back to St. Louis, and once again his connections and fast talking got him out of prison. In August he led a small group into Huntsville, falsely claiming to be under orders to restore order. He and his men did just the opposite, drunkenly bullying people until the local authorities fined them for disorderly behavior and made them leave town.

And that was the last that history records of Jacob Terman, alias Harry Truman. He seems to have disappeared off the face of the earth, although more likely he simply took on another name and went away to disturb another state. He had been an embarrassment to the Union cause in Missouri, and no doubt his commanders did not look for him very hard. They probably breathed a collective sigh of relief and prayed the name Harry Truman would never be heard in Missouri again.

Wild Bill Hickok's
Springfield Shootout
The Wild West's First Gunfight

It started like it always does in the movies—an argument in a saloon, two gunfighters threatening one another, one man swears vengeance, and later in the town square they draw their six-shooters and fire.

Yes, just like in the movies, except the movies hadn't been invented yet.

By 1865 Wild Bill Hickok was already famous in the West. He'd spent years as an Indian fighter and scout, did a stint as a town marshal, and had been in more than a few scrapes. He was feared for his skill with a gun and his knowledge of the vast countryside of the Old West. With his fine features, flowing hair, and muscular frame, he was as handsome as he was deadly.

He carried a pair of ivory-handled Colt .36-caliber US Navy pistols in his belt, and as holdout weapons a pair of .41-caliber Williamson derringers, tiny pistols that were nevertheless lethal at short range, such as across a poker table. He knew how to use them too. While the newspaper and dime novel claims that he had killed hundreds of men were no doubt exaggerated, even

47

Wild Bill Hickok wearing buckskins
Used by permission, State Historical Society of Missouri, Columbia

his most conservative biographer estimates he killed about ten men in seven authenticated shootouts.

Hickok was practical when it came to gunfights and kept a cool head, something that was far more important than speed. He once advised an acquaintance to aim for the navel.

"You may not make a fatal shot," he said, "but he will get a shock that will paralyze his brain and arm so much that the fight is all over."

There was just one thing that kept him from being the stereotypical Western hero: He was really bad at cards.

Hickok loved to play cards but had neither skill nor luck. On the night of July 20, 1865, in Springfield, Missouri, Hickok was, as usual, playing cards and he was, as usual, losing. His opponent was David Tutt. The two had an uneasy friendship. They had been on opposite sides of the Civil War, Hickok acting first as a Union teamster, then as a scout, and eventually as a spy, while Tutt had served the Confederates as either a sharpshooter or a scout, depending on what source you believe. That didn't really seem to trouble the two, however. What did trouble them were their frequent gambling and the fact that Hickok was a sore loser. Time and again they argued, fell out, buried the hatchet, and gambled again, starting the cycle anew.

At the end of another unsatisfying session for Hickok, Tutt reminded him that he owed him $45, a fair amount of money for the time. Hickok said that the original amount was only $35 and that he had recently paid Tutt $10, so he only owed $25. Upon hearing this, Tutt picked up Hickok's watch, which was lying on the table between them, and said he could have it back when he paid the outstanding $35.

Hickok was furious. The next day the two met, and one of their mutual friends tried to calm matters down. The man got Tutt to agree to return the watch if Hickok paid $35, but Hickok refused to pay anything more than $25, at which point Tutt went back to demanding the original sum of $45.

Both Tutt and Hickok agreed they didn't want trouble between them, with Wild Bill saying, "You have accommodated me more than any man in town. I have borrowed money from you time and again and we never had any dispute before in our settlement."

The two then went off to drink together, but the issue of the money still loomed over them like a dark cloud. After they finished their drinks, Tutt left the saloon, passed through the courthouse square, and went into another saloon. Hickok soon appeared at the corner of South Street and the square, telling anyone who'd listen that Tutt had his watch and that he better not try to recross the square while carrying it.

At 6:00 p.m. Tutt appeared on the opposite side of the square by the courthouse. Hickok approached, entering the square and yelling, "David, you cannot cross this square and pack my watch!"

Both men stopped and immediately drew their pistols. They stood about seventy-five yards apart. It's unclear who drew first, because all the eyewitnesses were behind Hickok, so they could clearly see Tutt but not what Hickok was doing. Whoever drew first, the other quickly followed suit, because the shots were almost simultaneous.

Tutt turned to the side to make himself a smaller target and fired. His shot went wild and Hickok, bracing his pistol on his left arm, squeezed the trigger and plugged Tutt right through the body.

Tutt staggered away, passing through one of the courthouse arches and then turning back onto the square before falling dead.

Hickok immediately spun around to the astonished crowd, which included several of Tutt's friends. None drew their weapons, but one man got up the courage to comment that what Hickok had done was "rather hard," to which Wild Bill replied, "It's too late now and I am not sorry."

A marshal soon arrived. Hickok allowed himself to be disarmed and arrested. He was charged with manslaughter, posted bail, and stayed in Springfield until the matter came to court.

The trial of James Butler Hickok was a media sensation. While Hickok and Tutt hadn't let their war records get in the way of their gambling, everyone noted that, only a year after the end of hostilities, a Union veteran and a Confederate veteran had gotten into a shootout. Former rebels were barred from the legal professions or serving on juries at that time, so the judge, both lawyers, and the jury were all Unionists.

The case had important legal ramifications. For many years duels had been illegal in Missouri. To shoot someone in a duel was considered a premeditated act of murder. Even in a nonconsensual fight, one was expected to retreat as far as possible and only fire upon the assailant if there was no other choice. But the increase in personal violence accompanied by the increase in the carrying of pistols led to a change in the law. For example, the Missouri Supreme Court ruled in the 1858 case of *State of Missouri vs. Epperson* that a man didn't have to wait until the assailant aimed a gun at him; rather, merely pointing a pistol in the general direction of the person allowed that person to fire in self-defense. The following year in the case of *State of Missouri vs. Hicks*, the court ruled, "When danger is threatened and impending we are not compelled to stand with our arms folded until it is too late to strike, but the law permits us to act on reasonable fear."

Whereas before, someone who felt threatened had a duty to retreat, now that person could stand and fight if he felt retreat wasn't a safe option.

Hickok's defense attorney argued the shooting was in self-defense, that Tutt was known as a dangerous thug, and that he had drawn first. The prosecuting attorney argued that Hickok helped bring on the fight and ignored their mutual friend's attempt to resolve the dispute before it escalated into violence. Bringing on a fight nullified the idea of self-defense. While the prosecution had a strong case, the jury found in favor of Hickok and found him not guilty.

Many in Springfield disagreed with the verdict, saying Hickok was looking for a confrontation. Hickok himself didn't deny it. When he ran for mayor later that year, he lost, partially because of the unpopularity arising from his shootout with Tutt.

While he lost prestige in Springfield, the gunfight launched him to fame. An exaggerated version of the gunfight and his life was written up in *Harper's*, a leading national magazine. Hickok became an instant celebrity and admirers and toughs flocked to him, either to badger him for stories of his adventures or to challenge him to fights to prove how tough they were.

Hickok soon left Springfield and tried to leave the shooting behind him. He worked as a lawman in a couple of places and as a scout for the US Cavalry, and traveled all over the West getting into scrapes and trying his luck at the poker table. His fame dogged him wherever he went, and he could never come to terms with it. While it appeared to annoy him, he accepted a job with a Wild West show in the eastern states, probably because of the high pay. It was universally agreed that he was a terrible actor and appeared to suffer from stage fright. His handsome appearance and his trick shooting were popular with audiences, however, and his manager was disappointed when Hickok said that he had had enough and went back West. A second attempt to make a stage career in Buffalo Bill's Wild West show also ended in disappointment.

The year 1876 found Hickok prospecting for gold in the Black Hills of Dakota as part of a gold rush. He spent a lot of time in the local town of Deadwood trying, as usual, to make money playing cards. He still didn't have much luck with it.

On August 2 he was sitting at the poker table with some friends in the No. 10 Saloon when Jack McCall walked in, pulled out a pistol, and shot him in the back of the head. To this day, just why McCall murdered Hickok is a mystery, but it led to one final story in the Hickok legend. When Hickok slumped over, his cards fluttered out of his hand. He had two aces, two eights, and another card that varies depending on which story you believe. Ever since that day, "Aces and Eights" has been known as the "Dead Man's Hand."

Two pairs is one of the lowest hands in poker. Wild Bill's last hand was a loser.

Frank and Jesse James
Legendary Bandits

It had been a good day at the Kansas City Exposition. As night fell, a huge crowd headed for the gates after enjoying a day listening to brass bands, watching trick riders, trying to guess what bushel of corn or fat hog would win the farming contests, and stuffing themselves at the concession stands. It was September 26, 1872, and Missouri was at peace. The economy was improving after the long years of the Civil War, and everyone just wanted to have a good time. Well-fed and content, the crowds headed toward home.

But three riders rode through the throng in the other direction. Murmurs and a few laughs scattered through the crowd when people noticed the men wore checkered bandannas over their faces. Were they entertainers, or local kids up to some prank?

One man dismounted in front of the ticket booth, and to everyone's amazement the other two pulled out pistols and aimed them at the hundreds if not thousands of people around them. Anyone who had been laughing stopped immediately.

The man strode over to the ticket booth, reached his arm through the window, and grabbed the cash box. The ticket seller shouted a protest and ran out of the booth to grapple with the robber. One of the riders fired a shot, but the ticket seller ducked and the bullet hit the leg of a young girl standing nearby. The robber leapt into the saddle and the three rode off, the crowd parting before them in panic.

Kansas City had just been visited by the James gang.

Frank and Jesse James were born to Robert and Zerelda James on a farm near Kearney, Clay County. Robert was a highly educated Baptist minister and one of the founders of William Jewell College in Liberty. In 1850 he left his young family and set out for the gold fields of California, where he soon died. Zerelda kept the farm going and eventually married Dr. Reuben Samuel.

Despite having lost their father, the James boys seem to have had a happy childhood. They loved their new stepfather and lived on a prosperous farm tended by slaves, but they must have been aware of the growing tensions in the region. Pro- and antislavery factions fought it out along the border with Kansas to determine whether the territory would become a slave or free state. Abolitionist Jayhawkers often raided border counties in Missouri, and the James brothers probably knew some of their victims.

This fierce border war, known as "Bleeding Kansas," was the prequel to the Civil War, which started in 1861. By then Frank was eighteen and Jesse just fourteen. Frank promptly enlisted in the pro-Southern Missouri State Guard and fought in the early Confederate victories at Wilson's Creek and Lexington. While things seemed to be going well for Missouri secessionists in 1861, they would be kicked out of the state the following year after a series of bloody engagements that gave the Union control of Missouri. While the Confederates launched several large raids, they never seriously threatened to take Missouri again.

But the fight was far from over. Frank had contracted measles and been left behind during the Confederate retreat from Lexington. Union troops captured and paroled him, making him take an oath not to fight the Union before allowing him to go home. He lived there peacefully until 1863, when the Missouri government required all able-bodied men to enroll in a Union militia. This was too much for Frank. While he would take an oath not to fight, he would never fight for the North. Local authorities arrested him for failing to join up, but he managed to escape from the Liberty jailhouse and ended up joining the guerrilla band of William Clarke Quantrill. He would spend the rest of the war roving the countryside, making hit-and-run raids on federal outposts and destroying train tracks and telegraph wires. Quantrill's wasn't the only guerrilla band operating in Missouri, and these innumerable groups of bushwhackers would be the main rebel resistance in the state for the rest of the war. While the Union had taken Missouri, they had a great deal of trouble holding it.

Unfortunately for the James family, everyone knew Frank had broken his oath and was fighting for the South once again. They might have also suspected that Zerelda and Jesse paid close attention to federal troop movements and ran messages for the bushwhackers.

One day in May 1863 the Union militia showed up at the James farm. This was the same outfit that Frank would have joined if he could have stomached fighting for the North. The militia questioned Dr. Samuel about Frank's whereabouts, and when he said he knew nothing, they put a noose around his neck, threw the rope over a branch of one of the trees in his yard, and strung him up. Jesse tried to intervene, but they whipped him until he lay limp and bleeding on the ground. The militiamen, laughing and teasing Jesse's stepfather, let him drop and then hauled him up again. The tortured man finally admitted that Frank and his friends were camped nearby, so the militia left on a fruitless chase after them. The frustrated soldiers soon returned to drag Dr. Samuel off to jail and force Zerelda to take a loyalty oath in court.

After this treatment, the young Jesse asked to join Quantrill's guerrillas too, but they rejected him as too young. They also weren't impressed when he shot off the tip of his finger while cleaning a pistol, screaming "Dingus!" As a good Baptist boy, he wouldn't swear even when losing a finger. For the rest of the war, "Dingus" would be his nickname among the bushwhackers.

Jesse finally got a chance to join his big brother in the spring of 1864. By that time Frank rode with "Bloody Bill" Anderson, leader of a faction that had split away from Quantrill's outfit.

Jesse didn't get to stay with his brother long. That summer he snuck into the yard of a Unionist farmer to steal a saddle and the man shot him. The bullet pierced Jesse's chest and passed right through his body. This laid Jesse up for two months, but as soon as he could get back on his horse, he rode off to rejoin his brother, just in time for Bloody Bill's greatest killing spree. The band carved a crimson path through the state in support of General Sterling Price's raid in the autumn of 1864. Both brothers nearly got killed in a failed attack on a federal blockhouse in Fayette and went on to Centralia, where Anderson's band slaughtered twenty-two unarmed Union soldiers on furlough.

There is debate about whether Frank and Jesse were present for the Centralia Massacre, because much of the group stayed in camp that morning, but they were definitely present that afternoon when the bushwhackers wiped out a federal pursuit force. The gleeful guerrillas scalped and mutilated some of the dead, but there are no reports that the James brothers participated in this. Anderson got killed by a Union militia the next month, and Frank went to rejoin Quantrill.

After successive defeats on the field, the Southern cause seemed doomed, and Quantrill, one of the most wanted men west of the Mississippi, led his men east to Kentucky. It would not save him, however, and the Federals tracked him down and killed him. Frank went with him on that excursion, but managed to survive. Meanwhile Jesse raided around Missouri with another guerrilla group under the command of one of Anderson's former lieutenants.

As the war ended, the authorities in Missouri offered amnesty to bushwhackers who would surrender and take an oath of loyalty. Jesse spoke against surrender, but the other members of the band outvoted him. Deciding all was lost, he too rode toward Lexington to turn himself in, but before they made it to town, they got ambushed by federal troops. It's unclear why this happened; perhaps the troops thought they were one of the many bushwhacker groups who weren't surrendering, or perhaps they simply wanted revenge for all the suffering the guerrillas had caused. Missouri was chaotic at the time, and no one could tell friend from foe. In any case, Jesse had his horse shot from under him and took a bullet in his lung. Lying half dead in the Virginia Hotel in Lexington, he managed to raise his right hand and take the Oath of Loyalty on May 21, 1865. This action made him a rehabilitated rebel in the eyes of the federal government. Over in Kentucky on July 26, Frank took the oath as well.

Jesse took a long time to recover from the bullet that hit his lung and had to be nursed back to health by his cousin, who like his mother was named Zerelda. Jesse called her "Zee." As the former guerrilla lay recovering, the two fell in love and got engaged, although the wedding wouldn't happen for another nine years.

Frank, on the other hand, had more serious business to attend to. Apparently he couldn't adjust to peacetime life and on February 13, 1866, rode into Liberty with about a dozen men. They wore Union-style blue army overcoats, and some wore wigs and false beards and mustaches. Two of them walked into the Clay County Savings Association Bank, asking the cashier for change for a $10 bill. When the man turned to address them, he found himself staring at the business end of a pistol. They pushed the cashier and clerk into the vault and cleaned out the money before closing the vault door on them.

The robbers hadn't actually locked the door, however, and the cashier ran to a window to call for help as the bandits mounted up. Just then a student at William Jewell College, which Frank's father had helped found, passed by. He took up the call and one of the robbers shot him dead. They galloped out of town as the citizens of Liberty gathered a posse.

It was too late: The robbers were well ahead, and a snowstorm soon blew in and obscured their tracks. The gang got away with more than $57,000 in cash, gold, and government bonds.

The choice of the bank hadn't been random. Frank knew the area well, and the bank's president had been a Union informant during the Civil War, causing trouble for Dr. Samuel and friends of the James family. Liberty had another bank, but Frank had a score to settle with this one.

While Jesse has been said to have joined in the robbery, he was still recovering from his gunshot wound and unlikely to have been up for the job. He seems to have lived a quiet life at the time, joining the local Baptist church. Frank may or may not have engaged in other robberies in the state, but generally seems to have kept a low profile except for the occasional bender in town.

On a rather ominous note, in September 1869 Jesse made a formal request to be taken off the rolls at his Baptist church, saying he was unworthy.

In December of that year, Frank and Jesse committed what may have been their first robbery together. They and possibly one other man rode into Gallatin, hitched their horses in an alley near the Daviess County Savings Association, and walked inside. They shot cashier John Sheets before running to their horses. One of the men, probably Jesse, had trouble mounting up and got his foot caught in the stirrup. The horse dragged him down the street before he could break free. Battered and covered in dust, the robber staggered to his feet.

"Let's get him!" someone shouted, and an angry crowd closed in on him. He pulled out a pistol and the townspeople fled in all directions. The bandit vaulted onto the back of a companion's horse and they rode away.

Outside of town they came upon an unsuspecting traveler and relieved him of his horse, then kidnapped a traveling preacher to guide them for part of the way. The robbers boasted to him that they had killed Major Samuel Cox, who had led the militia that killed "Bloody Bill" Anderson near the end of the Civil War. The raid on Gallatin may have only been for revenge because, contrary to the first newspaper reports, apparently no money was taken.

Actually they had killed Sheets, thinking he was Cox, but their desire to kill Cox implicated the James brothers in the robbery. Both had ridden with Anderson. The third robber may have been Jim Anderson, another former bushwhacker and Bloody Bill's brother. The authorities traced the horse that one of the robbers left behind to Jesse James. Furthermore, a posse that went after them lost the trail but noted they were headed in the direction of Clay County, home of the James/ Samuel family.

Four men showed up at the James farm to capture them, but just as they arrived a young boy ran to the stable, opened the door, and Frank and Jesse galloped out, guns blazing. One of the posse's horses was killed and they lost the chase.

The James brothers laid low for a while, with Jesse writing to the newspapers protesting his innocence and saying he had fled because he didn't want to get lynched. The horse found at Gallatin, he claimed, had been sold to a "man from Kansas." Otherwise, they seem to have drifted from state to state. The law accused them of other robberies, but it is hard to separate fact from fiction. By this time the brothers had become famous, and any major heist usually got laid at their door. Furthermore, other bandits would claim to be them, either to enhance their reputations or direct suspicion away from themselves. So many stagecoach, train, and bank robberies happened at this time that they couldn't have all been done by the Jameses, but a few probably were, including the Bank of Columbia in Kentucky and the infamous heist at the Kansas City Exposition.

That last robbery, certainly their most daring, guaranteed their national fame. The editor of the *Kansas City Times*, an alcoholic ex-Confederate soldier named John Newman Edwards, turned the thieves into noble Robin Hoods out of some epic ballad, effusing, "These men are bad citizens but they are bad because they live out of their time. The nineteenth century with its Sybaric civilization is not the social soil for men who might have sat with Arthur at the Round Table, ridden at tourney with Sir Launcelot or won the colors of Guinevere . . . What they did we condemn. But the way they did it we can't help admiring."

Edwards would continue in this vein throughout the James brothers' careers, and his paper often received letters from the bandits themselves. Sometimes they would sign their own names, claiming their innocence. At other times they signed themselves "Dick Turpin, Jack Shepherd, and Claude Duval," famous English highwaymen from the previous century. They even offered to pay the medical expenses of the girl they accidentally shot at the Kansas City Exposition. It's not recorded if her family ever took the robbers up on their offer.

In 1874 the gang resurfaced in Arkansas, robbing a stagecoach at Malvern before heading north to hold up a train at Gads Hill, Missouri, pulling off the state's first peacetime train robbery. This last crime got the Pinkerton detective agency on their trail. The Pinkertons had gained a reputation for success in tracking down outlaws, and the railroad hired them to get the James brothers in case they decided to repeat their trick on another train.

While the Pinkertons claimed to be crack detectives, they didn't go about collaring Frank and Jesse James in a very intelligent manner. At first only a single agent, Joseph Whicher, went off to the James farm, posing as a farmhand looking for work. He must not have been very convincing, because his body turned up in another county. Next they sent two more agents, along with a local deputy sheriff, but the Younger brothers, former bushwhackers and accomplices of Frank and Jesse, got to them first and killed the deputy and one of the agents.

All this bloodshed didn't seem to affect Frank's and Jesse's personal lives much. On April 24, 1874, Jesse finally married his beloved Zee, and Frank married Annie Ralston sometime later that summer. The two couples enjoyed a fine honeymoon in Texas with their stolen money.

But things started heating up for the brothers. Their daring robberies had become a political issue, with the Republicans demanding they be brought to justice, while the Democrats, mostly made up of former Confederates, pointed out that corrupt Republican politicians and railway tycoons stole far more than the James brothers could ever dream of. Reward money, offered by the railroads, various banks, and eventually the state, began to pile up.

Unlike the politicians, the Pinkertons didn't just talk. They had lost two agents and wanted revenge. On the night of January 25, 1875, a group of Pinkerton detectives snuck up to the James farm, thinking the bandits were inside. Actually, only their stepfather Dr. Samuel, their mother Zerelda, and their thirteen-year-old half-brother Archie were at home. The lawmen broke open a window and tossed in an incendiary device. It rolled into the fireplace and exploded, killing Archie and mutilating Zerelda's hand so badly that it had to be amputated.

The Pinkertons claimed they were "only" trying to burn the house down, but the senseless killing of a young boy and the maiming of an aging woman enraged the population. The Pinkertons worked for the railroads, the corrupt companies that overcharged farmers for freight and had put dozens of counties deep into debt. Edwards and other newspapermen wrote scathing editorials denouncing the Pinkertons as child killers. Sympathy for the James brothers rose to an all-time high. One of their neighbors, who apparently helped out in the raid, turned up dead.

While Frank and Jesse had become legends in their own time, law-abiding citizens began to stock up on guns and get ready in case the outlaws visited their town next. The brothers would find their heists becoming increasingly dangerous. When Frank James, Cole Younger, Tom Webb, and Tom McDaniel hit a bank in Huntington, West Virginia, netting more than $10,000 in cash, a posse got on their trail right after they left town. The robbers fled into Kentucky, where a second posse chased them halfway across the state while the telegraph wires hummed across the countryside, warning citizens to be on the lookout. They fought at least three gun battles, and McDaniel got killed before the rest made good their escape.

Worse was to come in 1876 when the James brothers once again teamed up with the Younger brothers to raid a bank in Northfield, Minnesota. Northfield citizens greeted them with a hail of gunfire, and Frank and Jesse barely got away with their lives. The Youngers got the worst of it; the bloody shootout is detailed in the following chapter about their exploits.

The Northfield affair badly shook the brothers and their new wives. They decided to take on aliases and settle as farmers in Tennessee. Mr. and Mrs. Woodson (Frank and Annie) and Mr. and Mrs. Howard (Jesse and Zee) did well for a time, racing horses and tending crops, but they acted too differently from their run-of-the-mill neighbors to escape notice for long. People began remarking that the men seemed a bit jumpy and that the women had a lot more jewelry than people of their station would be expected to have. In one episode, Jesse James/John Howard attended a county fair and watched a contest where men tried to blow out a candle by shooting at it with pistols. As contestant after contestant missed the mark, Jesse could stand it no longer and went up, drew his revolver, and shot out the candle on the first try. Jesse, always more showy than his quiet and reserved brother, was beginning to make people talk. This, combined with various lawsuits from creditors, made him pick up stakes and move in with Frank.

But settled life didn't sit well with Jesse, and soon he headed down to New Mexico Territory to assemble another gang. He briefly tried to get Billy the Kid to join, but Billy preferred cattle rustling to bank robbery and turned him down. Jesse did manage to collect a group of outlaws, but of inferior quality to the old crew. They included Bill Ryan, who had no previous criminal record and spent much of his time drunk; Dick Liddil, a horse thief; Tucker Bassham, a slow-witted farmer; Ed Miller, brother of Clell Miller, who had died at Northfield; and Jesse's cousin Wood Hite. Another cousin, Clarence Hite, would join later. Their first holdup was of a train at the Glendale station, just south of Independence, where the express mail netted about $6,000. This heist led the United States Express Company to offer a $25,000 reward, and the Chicago and Alton Railroad offered another $15,000. With all the rewards that had accumulated on Jesse's head, anyone who nabbed him would be a rich man.

Things began to turn ugly for the new gang. Bassham got captured and sentenced to ten years for the Glendale robbery. Ed Miller died under mysterious circumstances, and everyone believed Jesse killed him so he wouldn't talk.

The gang continued to rob stagecoaches, trains, and payroll shipments, but often got away with very low stakes. Soon Ryan also found himself behind bars, after foolishly shooting off his mouth while on a bender. Jesse's earlier successes were due in no small part to the fact that he allied himself with former bushwhackers such as the Younger brothers whose skill and daring helped them get out of almost any scrape. Now Jesse kept company with lowlifes and amateurs. It would cost him.

Meanwhile, political pressure had been growing to do something about the new James gang. Missouri Governor Thomas Crittenden got the railroads to offer another $50,000 reward. State law prohibited Crittenden from offering a large reward himself, but he'd be a key player in stopping the gang's crime spree.

But by this time there wasn't much of a gang left to chase. Liddil got into an argument with Jesse's cousin Wood Hite and gunned him down for allegedly taking more than his share in a robbery. Two new gang members, Bob and Charlie Ford, were there too. Bob got into the gunplay and his bullet might have actually killed Jesse's cousin. The three men dreaded what Jesse might do if he found out.

The Fords decided to stay close and watch Jesse's every move. Hiding out first in St. Joseph and then at the James farm near Kearney, the bandit leader planned more robberies, but Bob Ford had secretly met with Governor Crittenden, who promised him a rich reward for Jesse's capture. Bob claimed it was to bring in the bandit "dead or alive," something the governor would vigorously deny.

Soon Dick Liddil surrendered to police, and this made Jesse nervous. While he was still ignorant of Liddil's part in

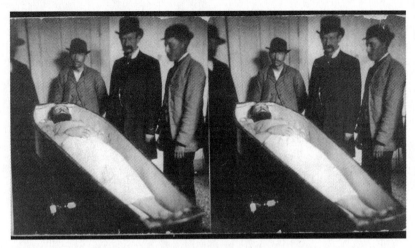

Jesse James lying in his coffin after being murdered by Robert Ford. When placed in a proper viewer, this stereoscopic image gives a 3D picture. Images like this were widely popular in the late nineteenth and early twentieth centuries. *Courtesy Library of Congress*

his cousin's murder, he didn't trust him and worried he might talk. Jesse discussed killing Liddil and acted more and more suspicious of those around him. Bob and Charlie Ford realized they needed to get him soon.

They got their chance on April 3, 1882, as the Fords and Jesse sat in the living room in Jesse's home in St. Joseph. Jesse complained about the heat and took off his coat and threw open the windows. Worried someone outside might see his gun belt, he took that off too. Then he stepped onto a chair to dust a picture on the wall. Bob gave Charlie a wink and they both drew their pistols. Jesse heard them cock their revolvers and began to turn just as a single shot from Bob's gun took Jesse in the back of the head. He fell to the floor, dead in an instant. Zee raced into the room, and Charlie claimed that a pistol had accidentally gone off.

"Yes," she snapped, "I guess it went off on purpose."

The Fords beat a hasty retreat and turned themselves in to the law. Within hours of the news being made public, a stream of visitors came to the James farm to view the body of America's most famous outlaw. The Fords were initially charged with murder but gained a pardon from Governor Crittenden.

The press, of course, took sides. The Democratic papers, led by John Newman Edwards, railed against Crittenden, calling him an assassin. The Republican press was just as eager with their praises for the termination of the state's worst outlaw.

Frank, meanwhile, was still living the quiet life in Virginia. He hadn't participated in a robbery in several years, and hoped this clean living would help him get pardoned. He sent out feelers to Governor Crittenden via Edwards, and the newspaperman reassured him that if he gave up, he would be given a fair trial and not be extradited to other states to face charges there.

Frank decided to take a chance and turned himself in to the governor, handing over his pistols and telling him he would fight no more. People thronged to see the famous outlaw, and when he went to trial he was found innocent of all charges. His case was helped by the fact that so many fellow gang members, the only ones who could truly say what he had done and when, were dead or on the run. The cases may have also been helped along by the governor himself, who felt convinced that Frank had turned over a new leaf and simply wanted the whole affair to be over. Frank walked out of jail a free man.

While the legend of Frank and Jesse James had been made in their lifetime, with cheap novels about their exploits being published while they were still out robbing banks, it would continue to grow to the present day, helped in no small part by those involved. Frank eventually joined Cole Younger in a Wild West show, and Jesse's son, Jesse James Jr., would make a silent Western movie in which he played his father. This would be followed by dozens of others, few having anything to do with the real story. Charlie and Bob Ford even toured with a theater troupe, playing themselves in a production called *The Killing of Jesse James*. In one performance they were booed offstage to the shouts of "Murderers!" and "Robbers!"

Frank and Jesse's mother, still living on the James farm, buried Jesse in the yard and erected a fine monument over his grave. She sold tickets to tour the farm, regaling visitors with tales of Jesse and Frank's nobility and the evils of the Pinkertons. One stop on the tour was Jesse's grave, where she offered pebbles from the grave at a quarter apiece. When the supply got low, she'd go to a nearby creek and gather more.

A distinctly American bandit has been remembered in a distinctly American fashion, through tourism, mass media, and show business.

Cole Younger
Reformed Killer

Northfield, Minnesota, was a pleasant, peaceful town, but nothing special. About thirty miles south of St. Paul, it had a small college and acted as the trading center for the rich farmland around it. Its bank, the First National, wasn't particularly rich, but it held a certain attraction for a certain band of outlaws from Missouri.

The bank president was Adelbert Ames, a former Union officer and son-in-law of the hated Union general Benjamin Butler. Butler had achieved notoriety during the occupation of New Orleans when a Southern belle emptied a chamber pot over a Union soldier's head. The general announced that if any other women did this, they would be treated as "ladies of the evening plying their avocation." This insult to Southern womanhood brought a censure from the Confederate government and a brisk trade in chamber pots with Butler's face on them. But for the infamous James-Younger gang, made up of former Confederates, it would bring a lot more. Butler was said to have a lot of money in the First National, so robbing them would be like robbing the Union officers who helped win the war.

On September 7, 1876, the gang rode into town. It included Frank and Jesse James, Bill Stiles, Charley Pitts, Clell Miller, and the Younger brothers—Cole, Jim, and Bob. As Pitts, Bob Younger, and Frank James entered the bank, the others stayed outside, keeping a sharp lookout for the law.

This family portrait shows Henrietta Younger with three of her sons—from left to right, Robert, James, and Cole. *Courtesy Library of Congress*

What they weren't looking for, however, was an ordinary citizen named J. S. Allen, who walked through the small crowd of sentries and tried to enter the bank. Miller grabbed him and pulled out his gun, ordering him to keep still. Panicked, Allen ran off screaming, "Get your guns, boys! They're robbing the bank!" Nearby, a young medical student named Henry Wheeler started shouting too. He ducked as Miller fired a shot over his head but kept on hollering. More shots followed as Miller and Cole Younger rode up and down the streets, popping off their pistols and ordering everyone inside.

Meanwhile, the three robbers inside the bank leapt over the counter and ordered the employees to fork over the cash. The employees informed the robbers that the safe couldn't be opened because it had a time lock. This was a bluff, but all three employees stuck to the story even after getting smacked around a bit. Finally the robbers swallowed the story, also failing to notice the main cash drawer with $3,000 in it, and satisfied themselves with whatever spare change was lying around, a princely sum of $26.70. One of the employees lost his nerve and sprinted for the rear door, Pitts chasing after him and blasting away with his pistol. He hit the employee once in shoulder, but the fellow made good his escape.

By this point that wasn't the only shooting going on. The robbers riding up and down the street hadn't intimidated the citizens of Northfield; they had enraged them. All of a sudden, gunfire erupted from around corners and out of windows. Clell Miller took a shotgun blast full in the face and toppled to the ground. Charley Pitts's horse reared as it got hit by a bullet, and Cole Younger got another in the hip, as well as some buckshot. Soon Bill Stiles fell to the ground with a gunshot through the chest.

Henry Wheeler, who had narrowly escaped getting shot by the outlaws, grabbed a gun and ran to an upstairs window. The medical student took careful aim at Miller, who had unsteadily remounted as blood flowed from his ravaged face, and gunned him down.

The bandits inside the bank shot the cashier dead and rushed out, just in time to make new targets for the citizens of Northfield, who had even begun to throw rocks at the outlaws. Wheeler, who proved to be an excellent shot, hit Bob Younger in the arm. One of the James brothers got hit in the leg. The outlaws scrambled to their horses and galloped off, ducking low in their saddles as they were chased out of town by a hailstorm of lead.

But their ordeal wasn't even close to being over.

They were short one horse, and had to make do by stealing a plow horse from a farmer. This animal wasn't nearly as fast as the one that had been shot back in Northfield, and it would slow them down considerably. They continued their flight, but telegraph operators alerted the entire region of the failed robbery. In every town men loaded their guns and saddled up.

The first of these posses didn't do so well. At Shieldsville, about fifteen miles from Northfield, a group of vigilantes gathered in the local saloon to have a drink before they left. As they toasted themselves and bragged about how famous they would be when they caught the robbers, the gang rode up outside. Bob Younger, his arm dripping blood, passed out and flopped off the saddle. An old man in front of the saloon thought this looked a bit suspicious, and didn't buy the outlaws' explanation that Bob was a captured horse thief. He went inside and summoned the posse, who came out to find themselves facing drawn revolvers. They'd found the outlaws all right.

Despite having their guns at the ready, the outlaws were almost as scared of the posse as the posse was of them. The robbers threw Bob over his horse and galloped out of town, forgetting to take any horses or even the posse's guns. The posse stood around stunned for a few minutes until another posse arrived in town. With these reinforcements, and perhaps a few more drinks at the saloon, they thundered off after the gang, confident once again of their place in history. They caught up with them a few miles outside of town and exchanged some shots, but the bandits disappeared into the woods just as the sun was setting.

The next day dawned cold and drizzling. The James-Younger gang, weary, hungry, and bloodied, slogged westward. They stole some more farm horses, but these proved too slow and eventually they decided to ditch them and proceed on foot, reasoning that their pursuers would be looking for mounted men. But the rain persisted, and on foot they made even poorer time than before. They kidnapped a local farmer to act as a guide but soon let him go when he promised not to tell anyone their location. The farmer, of course, went straight to the nearest posse.

At this point the outlaws' nerves had become raw. They had been on the run for several days, sleeping in the woods or in haystacks, and eating whatever scraps they could steal from farmhouses. The James brothers complained that Bob Younger slowed them down and suggested they abandon him. When Bob's brothers angrily refused, Frank and Jesse James took off by themselves. They stole a horse and riding double managed to slip back to Missouri.

On September 21, a full two weeks after the Northfield raid, seventeen-year-old Axle Oscar Sorbel and his father Ole were milking their cows in their farmyard when Jim Younger and Charley Pitts passed by. Axle's father paid no attention, but the teenager noticed the men's boots had worn out so badly that their toes stuck out. He immediately realized these were two of the robbers who had worn out their boots on the long walk from Northfield. He got three neighbors to rush up to the top of a nearby hill to keep a lookout. They spotted the robbers heading into a nearby copse, and Axle rode to the nearby town of Madelia and raised the alarm.

Soon a large posse closed in on the woods where the bandits hid. When the outlaws fired on them, the Minnesotans sent volley after volley into the underbrush, keeping up a steady fire for an hour until no more shots came from out of the woods. They sent a group ahead to see if any were still alive. Bob Younger rose from behind some cover and said weakly, "I give up." His brother Cole had taken ten pellets of buckshot in his body—but still lived. Jim Younger had taken a nasty shot in the jaw, which knocked out five of his teeth and left him in excruciating pain. Charley Pitts lay dead. All were out of ammunition.

The locals hauled the Younger brothers off to jail, where the judge found them guilty of the robbery and the murder of the cashier and sentenced them to life in prison. It was the end to a career in crime almost as daring as that of Frank and Jesse James.

Unlike a lot of Missouri outlaws, the Younger brothers came from a respectable background. The Youngers were a wealthy family in Harrisonville, Cass County. Their father, Henry Younger, served as the first mayor of the town and owned large tracts of land and a fine house. He named his four sons Cole, Bob, Jim, and John. Cole, the eldest, remembered they "were given the best education the limited facilities of that part of the West then afforded" and "were reared in ease." Cole became an avid hunter and a good shot from a very early age.

In his autobiography, which is not always terribly factual, Cole claimed he fought for the Confederacy at the Battle of Carthage in Missouri on July 5, 1861. There is no independent verification for this, but that winter he certainly did get involved when he attended a party hosted by a Southern sympathizer. Since the guests were secessionists too, the party attracted the attention of the local Union militia, which showed up uninvited. Their captain made passes at the women, despite being already married, and tried to get Cole's sister to dance. She refused and the Union officer turned to Cole and demanded to know the location of the notorious guerrilla William Clarke Quantrill. He suspected Cole was one of the Quantrill's spies. When Cole replied that he didn't know, the Union officer called him a liar, not something a man of good reputation could let go unpunished. Cole knocked him down. The captain rose, drawing his pistol, but some of the other guests intervened. Cole hurried his sister back home and went into hiding.

The enraged captain had Cole charged with spying, a shooting offense. If Cole hadn't been a guerrilla before, he certainly became one now. He soon joined Quantrill's outfit and became one of its best fighters.

Cole Younger's father, despite being a Unionist and a businessman with government contracts, was murdered by the federal militia. Henry owned slaves, the militia reasoned, so therefore he must be a rebel. In actuality he, like most Missourians, was a "Conditional Unionist," meaning he wanted to avoid war but preserve slavery.

Nor did the militia have mercy on Henry Younger's widow. They harassed her so much that she moved with her four youngest children from Harrisonville to a farm the family owned in Cass County, but the militia showed up one night during a snowstorm and ordered her to set fire to her own house. She begged to be allowed to wait until morning for the sake of the children. The militia agreed, and at dawn put a torch in her hand and made her burn down the family home. She then led her children and a slave back to Harrisonville through the cold and snow. Cole wrote later that the trek ruined her health, and he never forgave the Union men of Missouri. His little brother Jim would later follow him into war and become a battle-hardened veteran.

Despite all the indignities the Union heaped upon him, Cole was one of the more benign members of Quantrill's gang, often convincing the bloodthirsty guerrilla leader to let people go, although he did his share of killing in the Lawrence Massacre. Cole Younger eventually left Quantrill's gang sometime during the winter of 1863–64, when the guerrilla leader's power began slipping away. It's not quite clear what Cole did during this time, but the end of the war found him in California.

He eventually drifted back to Missouri and teamed up with his old comrade-in-arms Frank James to rob a bank in Liberty, making history with the first daylight bank robbery in peacetime. Soon his younger brothers wanted in on the action and while they rarely all worked together, when the James gang rode out for a heist, one or more Youngers usually rode along to help. Cole was the most capable, having had lots of practice shooting and riding during his war years.

The Youngers proved to be valuable allies in 1874, shortly after the gang robbed a train at Gads Hill. Two agents from the Pinkerton Detective Agency and a local deputy sheriff started searching for the gang in St. Clair County, one of the Youngers' hideouts. Only Jim and John were in the area, but that proved more than enough for the lawmen. On March 17 they found the outlaws, or more accurately the outlaws found them.

The Pinkerton agents and the deputy rode through the countryside, posing as cattle buyers and keeping a sharp eye out for the bandits and their known friends. Soon they came knocking at the door of an old farmer who happened to be sheltering the Youngers. As the Youngers hid, listening with pistols cocked, the farmer talked to the lawmen. He eventually sent them on their way, and Jim and John mounted up and followed them.

They caught up with them just down the road, and when the three lawmen turned in their saddles, they found themselves facing Jim's revolver and John's double-barreled shotgun. One of the Pinkertons dug his spurs into his horse's flanks and galloped off. The brothers fired on him, shooting off his hat, but he made it safely away, leaving his compatriots to their fate.

The other two tried to bluff their way out, sticking to their cattle buyer story. Jim and John Younger didn't swallow it, however, and disarmed them. When it became obvious the lawmen would be executed, the remaining Pinkerton agent whipped out a concealed pistol and shot John in the neck. John let loose with both barrels of his shotgun, tearing through the agent's arm. On reflex Jim shot the deputy, who all this time had been sitting quietly in his saddle. The Pinkerton agent galloped down the road, and the dying John thundered after him, drawing a pistol and giving the agent a mortal wound before the blood loss from his neck caused him to lose consciousness, and soon his life.

The Pinkertons had proved no match for even part of the James-Younger gang, and the outlaws remained free to continue their crime spree until the failed Northfield raid ended the Youngers' career, and ended the greatest gang of outlaws the country had ever seen. Jesse James went on to form a new gang—but with men of inferior quality who ended up betraying him. Cole, Jim, and Bob Younger became model prisoners, working at various jobs and hoping someday to be paroled. Bob died in prison in 1889.

While it is often said of criminals that their past will eventually catch up with them, in Cole's case this turned out to be a good thing. Years before, he had been standing picket duty after he and Quantrill's band had participated in the Confederate victory at the Battle of Lone Jack, and met a Confederate major named Warren Bronaugh. Cole warned Bronaugh that he was headed in the wrong direction and that if he continued down the road, he would run right into a large number of federal troops. Bronaugh never forgot the man who saved his life, and when he realized the famous outlaw was the same man, he started an epic campaign to get his release, writing hundreds of letters to politicians and newspapers and urging the government to pardon Cole and Jim.

Bronaugh was not alone; even some of Cole's former enemies tried to help. Stephen Elkins, who had been one of Cole's schoolteachers, had the misfortune of being a Union sympathizer and getting captured by Quantrill's gang. That usually meant death, but Cole lied to Quantrill, saying Elkins had relatives in the rebel army. Elkins was now Senator Elkins of West Virginia, and added his connections and power to the movement for Cole's and Jim's release. Emory Foster, who was a Union major when he and his brother got captured by Quantrill's band, remembered Cole saving him from being shot by another guerrilla. Cole even went so far as to carry a thousand dollars of Foster's money to his mother in Warrensburg.

After a long campaign the two brothers got paroled in 1901, but with the condition that they didn't leave the state of Minnesota. They came out into the twentieth century, relics of the nineteenth. They had no friends in Minnesota and no real way to earn a living. Furthermore, Jim's body had wasted away in prison because his destroyed jaw forced him to survive on a liquid diet. Cole, on the other hand, had swelled into fat middle age because of poor prison food and lack of exercise.

Jim and Cole got hired as traveling tombstone salesmen, heading to remote towns and farms to sell their stock of gravestones from the back of a wagon. But irony does not breed success, and Jim got injured and could no longer work. Cole found he wasn't much of a salesman and had trouble making ends meet.

Jim, distraught at losing his job and being rejected by a woman, took his own life in 1902. Cole got a full pardon the next year, which allowed him to return to his beloved Missouri. He and Frank James soon formed the "Cole Younger and Frank James Historical Wild West Show." One of the conditions of Cole's parole was that he couldn't display himself for monetary gain, so he worked as the business manager while Frank did skits, including one where he played a stagecoach passenger in a holdup, which must have gotten some laughs from the audience. The backers of the show turned out to be rather unsavory characters, and Cole nearly lost his parole when a number of employees got charged with gambling, cheating, and robbing ticket holders. The aging outlaws tried to get rid of the thieves, and in one incident they surrounded Frank and started threatening him. Frank spotted Cole nearby and reached for his gun, calling out, "Come in here, Cole, we've got a little cleaning up to do." The crooks learned some quick respect for their elders and took off running. Frank and Cole terminated their contracts soon after.

Cole ended his days on the lecture circuit, giving a rambling talk titled "What My Life Has Taught Me" on the evils of crime and the advantages of sobriety, clean living, and patriotism. He died in 1916, taking to his grave fourteen bullets and shotgun pellets that had never been removed from his body, testament to long years fighting for the South, and then fighting for money.

Belle Starr
Lady Legend of Lawlessness

In February 1863 Missouri was in the middle of a bloody Civil War. The Richey family of Newtonia was entertaining their honored guests, Major Eno of the Eighth Missouri Militia and his staff. Unlike many of their neighbors, the Richeys supported the Union and didn't mind having a Union officer as a guest. Just as they sat down to dinner, they saw a fifteen-year-old girl ride up. Her eyes and hair were remarkably dark, and she rode as well as a cavalry officer.

The girl introduced herself as Myra Maybelle Shirley of Carthage, but everybody called her "Belle." She said she'd lost her way and asked to stay the night.

Missourians rarely refused hospitality, even in those troubled times, and soon Belle sat with the rest of the group, chatting pleasantly with the officers. After dinner she played the piano for them. They felt at ease with this friendly, intelligent girl, and didn't notice that she took an inordinate interest in how many men they had and where they were billeted.

The next morning Belle thanked the Richeys for their hospitality and prepared to go. Before mounting up, she told them she wanted some switches for her horse. She cut two or three from a cherry bush out front and rode off, giving them a cheery wave good-bye.

Cutting the switches was a signal to rebel lookouts hidden nearby. Belle hadn't gotten far down the road when the woods around the home erupted in gunfire, bullets peppering the house. Major Eno and his men never used the Richey home as a base of operations again.

It was the first episode in the long adventure of the woman who became known as Belle Starr.

She was born on February 5, 1848, to the first hotel owner in Carthage. The hotel served as a refuge of fine dining in what was still very much a frontier town on the eastern branch of the Santa Fe Trail. The extensive library and the piano in the parlor added a touch of class, and the Shirleys were highly respected members of the community. Their children went to the best local schools.

The small, dark girl was extremely bright and did well in school, entertained guests with her considerable flair for the

Belle Starr on her horse in front of her home at Younger's Bend, in Indian Territory. The home provided safe refuge for her and her outlaw friends, becoming a veritable outlaw's hotel for many years. *Courtesy Oklahoma Historical Society*

piano, and seemed destined to become a leading member of polite society, but she also had a temper that could flare up at a moment's notice. She had no taste for feminine company and preferred to spend time with her older brother Bud, who taught her to ride and shoot.

Most members of the Shirley family were ardent secessionists, and when the war started Bud joined a band of local boys who harassed local Union forces, becoming one of the more successful, and therefore hunted, bushwhackers in Jasper County. In early 1864 he and a companion were eating dinner at the house of a Confederate sympathizer when a company of Union soldiers, working off a tip, surrounded the house. The two tried to escape by jumping over a fence, but Bud was shot and killed.

Distraught over Bud's death, the Shirley family moved to Texas, where they hoped the war wouldn't reach them. They settled on a farm outside Dallas, which at the time was booming because of Confederate trade with Mexico. The Union navy had blockaded all Southern ports, so the overland route to Mexico remained the Confederacy's only reliable contact with the outside world.

Belle was bored stiff. The one-room schoolhouse in the nearby village of Scyene had nothing to teach her she hadn't already learned in the female academy in Carthage, and there was nothing to occupy the fancy of a wealthy girl accustomed to being the center of attention at a bustling hotel. But soon she'd have more excitement than she had ever hoped for.

Belle's first brush with outlawry came when the James and Younger brothers stayed at the Shirley farm in 1866. They had just robbed a bank in Liberty, Missouri, and made off with a large number of gold coins. Since gold was rare in those days and could incriminate them, they came to the border to sell it to a Mexican banker for greenbacks. Cole Younger knew Belle's father from Missouri, so the gang used the farm as a safe haven. Many writers claim Cole and Belle fell in love during this time and Belle got pregnant. She'd later give birth to a daughter named Rosie Lee, nicknamed "Pearl," who many people called Pearl Younger. Modern researchers, however, say there's no evidence for the romance, and Cole himself wrote that he barely knew the girl.

A former bushwhacker named James Reed was probably Pearl's father. He and Belle married in 1866 and he moved to the Shirley farm, where Belle gave birth to Pearl two years later.

Belle spent many of the following months with Reed in Missouri, riding sidesaddle on fine horses and showing off her baby in the best clothes money could buy. Her husband roamed about, racing horses, gambling, and hiding out in the Indian Territory on his friend Tom Starr's ranch. Tom was the patriarch of the Starr clan of Cherokees, who had fought for the South during the war and sheltered the James and Younger brothers after several of their escapades. An old-time warrior, Tom Starr sported a necklace of earlobes cut from the men he had killed. He was also an outlaw, and teamed up with Reed to steal horses and cattle.

James and Belle Reed soon headed to California, bringing the one-year-old Pearl with them. One story says two brothers named Shannon killed one of James's brothers and James had exacted a bloody revenge, or it may have been an arrest warrant for selling whiskey to the Indians that made him leave. James worked in a gambling house in Los Angeles and Belle got pregnant again, giving birth to a son, James Edwin, nicknamed "Eddie."

Soon they returned to Texas, this time so James could escape a warrant for using counterfeit money. At first they tried to make it as peaceful farmers, but the lure of easy cash proved too much for James and he teamed up with one of his brothers to rob and kill a man. When they started to worry that one of their friends would turn them in, they killed him and cut out his tongue as a warning of what would happen to any other would-be stool pigeons.

James was now wanted in both Arkansas and Texas and had a $1,500 price on his head, so the young couple left their children with Belle's parents and fled to the Indian Territory, only to get into more trouble.

Police named James as a suspect in an 1872 robbery in which three robbers looted the ranch of a former judge of the Creek Tribe Supreme Court, making off with more than $30,000 and nearly killing the old man. Not long after that a gang held up a stagecoach headed to San Antonio, stealing about $4,000 from the mail and passengers in perhaps the first stagecoach robbery in Texas. The daring robbery received widespread coverage in the press, with Reed named as a prime suspect.

Sick of the wandering life and her husband's constant trouble with the law, Belle returned to her parents to take care of her children. Not only was her husband a criminal, but a greedy and incompetent one. His name was all over the papers, and she never saw a cent of his money. Reed and his accomplices spent it all on drinking and gambling in Dallas, once losing $3,000 on a single horse race.

But Reed had an appointment with the coroner. Deputy Sheriff John Morris, working undercover, befriended him and traveled with him for a time, waiting for the right moment to make an arrest. That moment came while they stopped for dinner at a ranch. Morris slipped out of the room, removed Reed's pistols from his saddle bags, then went back and pointed a gun at him.

"Jim, throw up your hands," he ordered.

Reed promised to go quietly, but then ducked down, overturned the table, and used it as a shield as he tried to run out the door. Morris fired twice, the bullets drilling through the thick wood. Reed dropped the table in panic, and Morris emptied his revolver into him.

Belle didn't mourn long. By 1879 she was whooping it up with Bruce Younger, half-brother of Cole Younger's father, in the mining town of Galena, Kansas. Apparently they made quite a pair, because they scandalized even the rough culture of that place. Bruce was a foul-mouthed gambler and made a stark contrast to the well-dressed Belle with her educated speech. Many writers made up breathless accounts of Belle dressing in men's clothing, or wearing outlandish outfits accompanied by such fashion statements as necklaces made of rattlesnake rattles, but all this seems to be an exaggeration. It's not clear whether they were actually married, but in that place and in those times, nobody much cared.

Whatever the status of Bruce and Belle, it didn't last long. Soon she returned to Tom Starr's hideout in the Indian Territory, where she fell in love with Tom's son Sam in 1880. This relationship lasted longer than the others, but caused Belle more trouble than the first two combined.

At first all went well. The couple settled on a patch of forest and bottomland on the banks of the Canadian River on the Cherokee Reservation. It was an isolated spot, partially screened by rough hills, surrounded by trees, and six miles from the nearest settlement. The only way to get to the cabin was through a narrow canyon that provided a perfect spot for an ambush. A pair of outlaws could ask for no better home.

It had another attraction. Local rumor said that the former resident, a Cherokee named Big Head, had buried $10,000 in gold somewhere on the property and died before revealing the location. The newlyweds spent a great deal of time digging around the place, making it look like the land was infested with prairie dogs.

The farm's isolation, the protection of the Starr clan, and the legal obstacles facing US lawmen trying to pursue criminals into the Indian Territory soon made it a popular hideout, virtually an outlaw's hotel, where fugitives found the Starrs' door always open and their mouths always shut.

Sheltering the likes of Jesse James wasn't the Starrs' only occupation. They also stole horses. In 1882 authorities charged both Belle and her husband with horse theft, and a posse headed out to catch them.

Friends tipped them off and the couple fled to the hills, but the lawmen tracked them down. Surrounded and outgunned, the couple had no choice but to surrender. As Belle screamed and cursed, the posse pulled a six-shooter out from her overskirt and two small derringers from the bosom of her dress. With their captives secured to a wagon, the lawmen set out on the long journey back to town. Belle amused herself by rummaging through the wagon's supplies and dropping out blankets, forks, and anything else she could grab, so when they made camp for the night, the deputies found themselves missing a lot their possessions.

One night she grew even bolder. While camped near Muskogee, the group went after some other criminals rumored to be nearby, leaving Sam and Belle under the care of a single guard. They put Sam in chains, but out of respect to the lady left Belle unsecured. As she sat eating inside her tent, a gust of wind opened up the tent flap and she spotted the sentry sitting with his back to her, the grip of his pistol enticingly within reach. She whipped it out of the holster and pointed it at him. Startled, he ran for it. Just then the rest of the posse showed up and witnessed Belle chasing the guard around the tent, a smoking revolver in her hand, him yelping as bullets whizzed by his head. Faced with the entire posse, Belle reluctantly gave up. They kept her chained after that.

During the trial the courtroom was packed with curiosity seekers wanting to see the novelty of a female horse thief. Her skill at riding had already made her famous in that part of the country, and she was rapidly becoming a legend in her own time, much like the James brothers, with all sorts of daring escapades attributed to her. Many claimed she had worked with James Reed and Sam Starr during all their robberies, toting a gun and dressing like a man. The court found both Starrs guilty, sentencing them to a year in jail, a remarkably lenient sentence for the time. Sam got hard labor, while Belle became the warden's secretary and tutored his children in French and music. Both went free after nine months for good behavior, and soon they were back on their farm and up to their old tricks. The outlaw hotel reopened for business.

Just before Christmas of 1884, the Starrs got one of their worst guests ever. John Middleton rode up on a stolen horse, a shotgun gripped in his hand and at least two murders to his name. He stayed at the ranch for some time, and the crime rate in the territory skyrocketed.

At this point John West, a local Indian policeman, decided to get tough on both Middleton and Sam Starr. He raided the ranch in the spring of 1885 and was greeted by Belle, who loudly cursed the lawmen and then laughed, saying they could never take Middleton. They searched the ranch anyway but didn't find the fugitives.

Despite her rough manner, the raid unnerved Belle, and she decided to take Pearl and Middleton to visit friends in Arkansas. They set out in their covered wagon, Middleton hiding in back. The outlaw soon got tired of the jolty ride and bought a stolen horse. He was found dead not long after, apparently drowned while crossing a swollen river. Among his possessions were Pearl's saddle and Belle's revolver—which convinced West that the Starrs were back to their old habit of harboring fugitives.

A local tale, completely unsubstantiated but too good not to tell, says one tenant at the outlaw hotel saw the teenaged Pearl sleeping in her bed and became entranced by her. He offered Belle $50 to sleep with Pearl. Belle took the money, stuck a pistol in his face, and said, "Now, you son of a bitch, get into bed and sleep with my baby, but if you so much lay a hand on her I'll blow your brains out." The outlaw gingerly crept into bed and spent a sleepless night balanced on the very edge of the mattress, praying Pearl didn't roll over in her sleep and touch him. Belle sat nearby, revolver at the ready, watching. Too stupid to learn his lesson, he complained to Sam about it the next day. Sam didn't have his wife's sense of humor and shot him in the arm.

John West's brother Frank, also a lawman, took a posse and followed Sam Starr's trail, finally catching up with him near the Canadian River as he rode through a corn field. Without asking him to surrender, Frank West fired at him several times, shooting the horse from under him and hitting Sam in the head. Triumphant, West and another man went to the nearest farm to get help while the other two guarded the unconscious outlaw.

While they were gone, Sam came to. Looking blearily around, he saw the guards had their backs turned. Despite the wound to his head, he leapt up, grabbed a gun out of one lawman's holster, disarmed the other, and rode away on one of their horses.

Sam celebrated his escape from justice by taking Belle to a Christmas dance. The hosts had an organ inside, and soon Belle sat down at the keys, playing expertly as couples swirled around the room. Sam hung around a bonfire outside with some others, passing the bottle. Then Frank West showed up. Sam Starr shouted at him for shooting the horse and both men drew their guns. Sam was the quicker draw and shot West in the neck. West staggered, recovered, shot Sam, and a moment later both fell dead.

After Sam's death, Belle's house stopped being an outlaw hotel. She wanted to live a peaceful life away from trouble.

But it was not to be. The Cherokee Nation wanted to take her land because her Indian husband was now dead. To avoid losing it, she shacked up with an adopted member of the Starr clan who called himself Jim July Starr.

Her troubles still didn't end. Pearl had now bloomed into a lovely girl of nineteen. Her belly bloomed too, and Belle got so enraged at her getting pregnant out of wedlock that she kicked Pearl out. Pearl moved away and eventually opened a bordello.

Belle's son Eddie, now seventeen, got arrested in 1888 for indulging in the family tradition of horse theft but got let go because he was dying of a head wound given to him by his accomplice for reasons unknown. He eventually recovered but hated the new man about the house. Soon he too became estranged from his mother.

To make ends meet, Belle began to lease out her land. A man called Edgar Watson, claiming to be from Arkansas, became one of Belle's sharecroppers. Belle sensed something wrong about him, and needled his wife for more information. The woman revealed that Watson actually came from Florida, where the authorities wanted him for murder. Belle evicted him, offering to refund his rent money, but he refused. Not to be deterred, she mailed it to him and gave the land to another. Watson told the new tenant that Belle would soon be arrested and scared him off, at which point Belle threatened to tell the Florida authorities what she knew. That would prove to be a fatal mistake.

On February 2, 1889, Jim July Starr rode to Fort Smith to answer the now-familiar charge of horse theft. Belle rode along for part of the way before heading back home. When she got to the store at King Creek, she looked glum. The storekeeper knew her well and asked her what was wrong. She replied that she feared getting killed.

"Why, Belle, thunder and lightnin' couldn't kill you!" the storekeeper laughed.

Belle didn't reply. Before she left, she cut her handkerchief in half and gave part of it to the merchant's wife as a keepsake.

Around 4:00 p.m. she made it to a friend's house, where several guests lounged about on the porch. One of them was her former tenant Edgar Watson, who had moved to a cabin nearby after Belle evicted him. He left as soon as he saw her. After talking with her friends for a time, she mounted up and headed home.

She didn't get far. As she rode past the Watson cabin, the blast of a shotgun tore through the air. Buckshot hit her in the back and neck and knocked her off the saddle. She painfully tried to lift herself from the ground, and got another blast at point-blank range in the shoulder and face. No one saw the murderer, but it didn't take a genius to figure out the culprit.

Belle received the most colorful funeral that part of the country ever saw. The Starr clan showed up in full force, along with numerous outlaws. A troop of heavily armed Indians carried her casket. Watson foolishly decided to go too. Just after the coffin was lowered into the ground, Jim July screamed at him, "You murdered my wife!" and only some quick intervention saved the funeral from becoming a gunfight.

Since all the evidence was circumstantial, the court found Watson not guilty of the murder, but justice caught up with him when he moved back to Florida and died in a gunfight there.

As with other outlaws, Belle Starr's reputation grew after her murder. The legend of the "Bandit Queen," the "female Jesse James," already gaining currency during her lifetime, grew into a nationwide obsession. She became the heroine of dime novels, ballads, plays, and eventually movies. Buried as she is in her own notoriety, it's hard to know what to make of her. At the very least she was a horse thief with terribly bad taste in men; at most she was one of the greatest female outlaws who ever lived.

The Bald Knobbers
A Second Civil War in the Ozarks

The Civil War died slowly in Taney County.

Most Ozark hill men fought for the South, but enough Unionists lived in the region to cause bitter infighting, and the federal army clamped down on rebellion with an iron hand. By the end of the war, Taney County had been nearly depopulated, dropping from 3,500 residents to less than 1,000. Many farms and homes were nothing but ashen ruins; even the county courthouse had been destroyed. Bankrupt and despondent, the local government could barely function.

When Confederate veterans returned home, many found their land occupied by Union men, confiscated for failure to pay taxes during the war. They couldn't even vote, thanks to a new state constitution that disenfranchised anyone who had supported the rebellion. Tension between the sides grew, and lawlessness grew with it. The impoverished county government could do nothing to stop the spiral into anarchy.

Things got a lot worse when Nathaniel Kinney arrived in 1883.

Standing six feet six inches and weighing 288 pounds, "Nat" Kinney was a giant of a man, broad shouldered and with incredible physical strength. He claimed to have been a decorated captain in the Union army, but military records show he never made it above private and contain no mention of any medals. He swaggered around the county capital of Forsyth, boasting about his heroics and showing off his two revolvers, which he called "Short Tom" and "Long Tom."

Kinney bought a large tract of land, where he opened a church with himself as preacher. From the pulpit he gave fiery harangues against criminals in the region, but some of the most regular attendants were local toughs who sat in the back rows, joking about this newcomer and how he'd never make them change their ways. They didn't know that Kinney had already started organizing a vigilante committee.

Lawlessness reached the breaking point with the killing of James Everett, owner of a grocery store and saloon and a well-respected citizen. On September 22, 1883, two customers were playing billiards at Everett's place while knocking back hits of moonshine. Soon the liquor got to their heads and one of them, Al Layton, accused his opponent of cheating. The argument descended into a brawl and Everett tried to kick them out. The other man left, but Layton drew his pistol and shot the saloonkeeper dead. He also wounded Everett's brother before stealing a horse and galloping away.

Layton eventually turned himself in. Despite there being plenty of witnesses, the court found him not guilty. People whispered that the jury had been plied with whiskey and that the county clerk, who was Layton's cousin, bribed the prosecutor.

But this wasn't going to be yet another case of a criminal going free. Everett had been one of Nat Kinney's friends and a regular at Kinney's vigilante meetings.

Shortly after Layton's acquittal, Kinney and twelve other prominent citizens met in the backroom of the Everett store. Most were Union veterans like himself, and half belonged to the Forsyth Masonic Lodge. One was Alonzo Prather, local attorney and publisher of *Home and Farm* newspaper, who later served five terms in the Missouri House of Representatives. Together they created a secret society reminiscent of the Masonic order, complete with initiation rituals, passwords, and a secret handshake. Their goal was to run lawbreakers out of the county.

The conflict had a political dimension as well. Taney County had been traditionally Democratic before the war, but the wartime exodus and the loyalty oath had kept Republicans in power afterward. The state abolished the oath in 1872, and the Democrats won control of the county government that same year. The government floated almost $18,000 in bonds to pay the county's debts, but it is unclear what exactly the money was used for. By 1884 the debt had ballooned to $42,000. Republicans accused the Democrats of embezzling, and some leading Democrats did seem to get suspiciously wealthy. Republicans also blamed them for looking the other way while friends and associates broke the law.

In the 1884 elections angry voters elected a slate of Republicans supported by Kinney's vigilante committee, kicking out Democratic incumbents for sheriff, treasurer, prosecutor, assessor, and, ominously, coroner. But Tom Layton, the Democratic county clerk everyone thought bribed the prosecutor during the Everett murder trial, kept his job.

Back in power, the Republicans summoned a state auditor to look at Taney County's finances, but before he could finish an unknown arsonist burned the new courthouse to the ground, taking the financial records with it.

Fed up, Kinney sent word to every man he trusted that he wanted them to join his new group. Recruitment turned out to be easy, because critics of the Democratic government, or even those who complained too loudly about lawlessness, found their livestock, crops, and barns destroyed.

The new recruits met on April 5, 1885, atop Snapp's Bald, a treeless hill offering a commanding view of the surrounding countryside. As many as two hundred men showed up and listened as Kinney gave a fiery speech, holding the bloody shirt of Jim Everett aloft and calling on all law-abiding citizens to avenge his murder and all other injustices. The men then took an oath of loyalty, swearing under penalty of death to keep their actions and identities secret. The group originally called themselves the Law and Order League, but two local jokers who saw the proceedings from a distance laughingly called them "Bald Knobbers" after the bare hill on which they met. The term stuck, and a name that started as a joke soon became the most feared words in the Ozarks.

The next night, the Bald Knobbers struck.

A hundred men, their faces covered with handkerchiefs or flour bags with eye holes cut in them, rode into Forsyth and surrounded the jail. They wanted Newton Herrell, awaiting trial for murdering his mother's lover. Rumor had it that he would walk free, and the Bald Knobbers wouldn't hear of it. Herrell saw the vigilantes coming through the bars of his cell window and lay on the floor, screaming so loud he could be heard half a mile away.

A detachment of masked riders rode off to the sheriff's house, but the sheriff refused to hand over the keys to the jail. The Bald Knobbers backed off, not wanting to hurt a lawman, and instead they draped a noose over the jailhouse door and judge's bench and rode off into the night.

Worse trouble came the next day.

A local tough named Frank Taylor sauntered into John Dickenson's store, demanding the owner give him some credit to buy a pair of shoes. Frank and his brother Tubal were notorious for galloping down Forsyth's main street shooting out windows. In fact, Dickenson should have felt grateful Frank didn't ride his horse into his store with a pistol in one hand and a bottle of booze in the other, his usual way of entering a place of business.

But circumstances had changed. Dickenson was now a Bald Knobber and defiantly told the troublemaker to leave. Taylor went berserk, wrecking the shop and walking out with a pair of shoes.

The following day, Frank, Tubal, and a friend appeared at Dickenson's store. Frank shoved a .32 revolver into Dickenson's mouth and fired, the bullet knocking out four teeth before exiting through his neck. Frank pushed the terrified man to the floor and put another bullet through his shoulder. The other two fired five shots at Mrs. Dickenson, shooting off the tip of her finger and grazing her neck. Both victims fainted and the attackers hurried away, thinking they had killed them.

This was too much even for Taney County. The Dickensons were respected and peaceful citizens who had moved there to join a socialist commune. The local government offered a $1,000 reward for the culprits, and Bald Knobbers fanned out across the countryside looking for them. The Taylors' accomplice ran off to Arkansas, where the authorities captured him, but the Taylor brothers got the bright idea of turning themselves in to some friends and dividing the reward. They had lived in Taney County all their lives, and since juries rarely favored newcomers over longtime residents, they felt they had nothing to fear.

They were wrong. The day after they went to jail, a hundred heavily armed Bald Knobbers showed up in town. While all covered their faces, everyone knew who led them. The huge man who swung a sledgehammer and knocked off the lock to the jailhouse door could be none other than Nat Kinney. The vigilantes dragged the screaming Taylor brothers outside, threw them over a pair of horses, and rode off.

It took some time for the residents of Forsyth to gather up the courage to follow. Two miles outside town they found the brothers hanging from the limb of a giant black oak. On Frank's shirt was pinned the cover of a shoebox with the message:

> BEWARE!
> These are the first Victims to the
> Wrath of Outraged Citizens
> More will follow
> THE BALD KNOBBERS

The lynching marked the beginning of a reign of terror. People who broke the law got whipped and threatened with hanging. Vigilantes burned barns and fields, and occasionally torched houses. Kinney and his followers waged a war for morality, punishing not only thieves and bullies but men who lived with women they hadn't married and men who beat their wives. "J'ine the band or leave the land!" became their rallying cry. They would warn a victim by throwing a bundle of sticks onto his porch. The number of sticks equaled the number of days the victim had to leave the area

But some refused to be intimidated. A group called the Anti-Bald Knobbers formed within a month, claiming *they* were the voice of law and order, but they remained indecisive, intimidated by the Bald Knobbers and limited in what they could do since they said they opposed vigilantism.

As people took sides, it became obvious the Civil War was being reenacted in the Ozarks. Many Bald Knobbers were newcomers, Republicans, and ex-Union soldiers. Virtually all had been born outside the county. Only a few kept farms, the main occupation of the general population, instead working in county government or the law, or owning their own businesses. They looked on native hill men as backward. The Anti-Bald Knobbers tended to be ex-Confederates and longtime residents, and most farmed for a living.

The ranks of the Bald Knobbers swelled, by some accounts getting as high as a thousand members. Attacks spread to those who owed the Bald Knobbers money or simply spoke out against them. The people they drove out of the county had to sell their land and livestock cheap, and usually a group of Bald Knobbers showed up to buy them. The victims could do nothing. Now it was the Bald Knobbers who controlled the courts and packed juries.

Through all this Kinney made no secret of being a member, even going so far as to grant newspaper interviews. To the *Springfield Herald* he said the fight was "a war between civilization and barbarism." He acted so publicly that he would announce meetings in the *Home and Farm* newspaper, but he never named other members.

Estimates of those killed by the vigilantes range from fifteen to more than thirty. Dozens got whipped, and no one is sure how many people were driven off their land.

But Kinney finally went too far when he killed a man named Andrew Coggburn. Coggburn's father had been killed in 1879 by men who would become Bald Knobbers and his family had been run off the land, but he didn't fear the vigilantes. Instead, he snuck up one night to spy on a meeting and laughed at rituals, going around town making fun of the Bald Knobbers to anyone brave enough to listen. This earned him a beating and a charge of disturbing the peace. He scoffed at the court and didn't appear. That got him a warrant for his arrest. Nat Kinney convinced the sheriff, a Bald Knobber, to deputize him so he could go after Coggburn himself.

When Coggburn next showed up at Kinney's church for his favorite activity of mocking the vigilante's sermons, Kinney pulled out a pistol and demanded he put up his hands. Some witnesses say he did, but others contend he only put up one hand and reached for his gun with the other. Whatever the truth, Kinney shot him dead. One witness, Sam Snapp, claimed Coggburn didn't even have a gun and that one was placed next to his body to make it look like Kinney fired in self-defense.

The next day the Anti-Bald Knobbers held an emergency meeting. They knew they wouldn't see justice prevail in the Forsyth courthouse, so they decided to organize an armed militia and appealed to Governor Marmaduke for help. Perhaps they hoped Marmaduke, a former Confederate general, would be sympathetic to their cause. They told him the county government was run by vigilantes and asked that their local militia be recognized. Kinney, sensing trouble, sent his own representatives to the governor.

Word of the bloodshed in the Ozarks had spread and Marmaduke wanted it stopped, no matter who had been on what side during the war. Marmaduke sent his adjutant general to Forsyth in April 1886 to meet with the rival factions. The adjutant told them both groups were illegal and had to disband, otherwise he'd send the state militia in to keep order. In a dramatic public meeting on April 11, Kinney made a show of formally dissolving the Bald Knobbers, but in reality the whippings and barn burnings continued. Some members claimed this was done by imposters, but few believed them. People began to hold prayer meetings calling on God to strike Kinney down with a bolt of lightning.

Kinney got worried. He hired a bodyguard, a veteran who had fought on both sides of the Civil War, and gave him the assignment to kill Sam Snapp, the eyewitness to the Coggburn killing. Kinney feared Snapp might testify or take revenge. The bodyguard followed Kinney's orders to the letter, gunning Snapp down in cold blood.

The Anti-Bald Knobbers had had enough. They held a secret meeting to decide which one of them would kill Kinney. Since pretty much everyone volunteered, they decided to play cards for the honor, with the man who got the low hand winning the prize of shooting Kinney. So they gathered around a table, playing the worst game of their lives, throwing out every decent card handed to them, until one man won. That man was Billy Miles.

It proved surprisingly simple. Miles spent some time pretending to be Kinney's friend, putting the vigilante leader at ease. Then all Miles did was walk into a store Kinney was tending in Forsyth, the same store that had been owned by Everett, whose murder had touched off the troubles. The day was August 20, 1888. Maybe Miles looked nervous, or the vigilante leader was smarter than the assassin thought, because Kinney suspected trouble and grabbed one of his guns. Miles was faster. His pistol blazed and a bullet shattered Kinney's arm. In agony, Kinney dropped his six-shooter, and Miles put another bullet through Kinney's heart. Amazed that he had downed the most dangerous man in the county and not trusting his luck, Miles put another three bullets into the corpse just to make sure Kinney was really dead.

Everyone hoped Kinney's death would end the reign of terror, and in Taney County it was, indeed, the beginning of the end. But a low level of violence continued between former members of the two groups, with a lynching as late as 1892.

The Bald Knobbers, of course, wanted revenge. They sent Taney County Sheriff Galba Branson and his friend Ed Funk, who they offered $1,500 to track down Miles, to the Kirbyville Fourth of July celebration after getting word that Billy Miles and his brothers Jim and Emanuel would be there. It would be the last trip they would take. The sheriff and bounty hunter cornered the three brothers down at a stream, but the Miles brothers filled Funk with lead. The sheriff managed to shoot Jim in the groin, but took a bullet to the head and died instantly. By then at least fifty men had their guns drawn and bullets were flying everywhere. Years of vigilantism had made everyone trigger happy.

The Miles brothers ran, afraid of some Bald Knobbers who were also attending the picnic. Soon more than a hundred armed vigilantes scoured the countryside. Jim, suffering miserably from his wound, eventually gave himself up, and lawmen captured Billy near Springfield. Emanuel got clean away, disappearing to parts unknown.

He needn't have bothered. Kinney's murder was ruled self-defense, as was the gunfight at the picnic. Public sympathy had turned against the Bald Knobbers.

A decline in the Bald Knobbers' popularity wasn't the only reason the fighting petered out. The Bald Knobbers, at least in Taney County, had pretty much won. Most of their opponents had fled, the rest cowed by Governor Marmaduke. The Republicans were firmly in control of Taney County and remain so to this day.

The violence, however, had spread. As outlaws fled Taney County, they ended up in neighboring counties, continuing to cause trouble and forcing locals to form their own chapters of the Bald Knobbers. Soon Bald Knobber organizations opened up in Douglas, Webster, Greene, and Laclede Counties.

The bloodiest fight happened in Christian County, where a local Bald Knobber chapter formed in opposition to two "blind tigers," unlicensed saloons operating illegally in Chadwick, the terminus of the recently completed Springfield and Southern Railroad. The vigilantes became active in the summer of 1886, led by David "Bull Creek" Walker. They raided the saloons, pouring the booze out on the street, and then, like their Taney County brethren, they went on to settle old scores and silence critics.

As public criticism grew and the group spiraled into lawlessness, Walker tried to disband, but instead his son Billy led the group on a raid on the cabin of one of their adversaries, killing two men in front of their horrified wives and children. The case drew national attention and the governor moved in. Dozens of Bald Knobbers went to trial. The jury heard how despite the fact that Dave Walker tried to stop them, after the attack he wanted to go back and kill the survivors, women and children included, and burn the cabin to the ground to hide the evidence. Several vigilantes received jail terms and three Bald Knobbers, including Dave and Billy Walker, went to the gallows.

It was a bloody end to one of the longest and bloodiest episodes of vigilantism in American history.

Did Jack the Ripper Live in St. Louis?
The Curious Case of Dr. Tumblety

For ten weeks in the winter of 1888, London was gripped with horror by a series of brutal killings. The victims were all prostitutes in the city's seedy East End.

Calling the East End a slum would be an insult to respectable slums everywhere. The area was overcrowded, its half-starved denizens crammed by the hundreds into filthy, rat-infested tenements. Raw sewage was heaped in the streets. While there were regular police patrols, there were virtually no street lights. Crime was rife and murderers were able to kill their victims only yards away from passersby without being seen.

At about 3:40 a.m. on Friday, August 31, the body of Mary Ann Nichols was discovered in Buck's Row in Whitechapel. She had had her throat cut with two deep slashes and had several cuts to the abdomen and two to her private parts. At 6:00 a.m. on Saturday, September 8, Annie Chapman's body was found in the backyard of 29 Hanbury Street, Spitalfields. She had been terribly mutilated, with her throat deeply cut and her abdomen ripped open and her intestines thrown over both her shoulders. Her uterus, part of her belly, including the navel, and parts of her vagina and bladder were missing.

The nature of the murders was savage even for the East End. Newspapers noted that the bodies hadn't been simply cut—they'd been ripped open. Soon the police were getting mocking letters from someone claiming to be the murderer and calling himself Jack the Ripper.

For a time the Ripper fell silent, and then on Sunday, September 30, he struck twice in the same night. Elizabeth Stride's body was found at about 1:00 a.m. in Dutfield's Yard, Whitechapel. She had been killed with a single deep cut to the throat. No other wounds were found, and it's theorized the Ripper was interrupted in his work and couldn't finish off his plan. To satisfy himself, he stalked another victim,

An illustration from *The Illustrated Police News* from October 6, 1888, depicting a man and a woman in an East End street. It's titled "Lured to the Slaughter." *Courtesy Museum of London*

Catherine Eddowes, whose body was found in Mitre Square in the City of London (a borough next to Whitechapel) just forty-five minutes later. This time the Ripper got what he wanted. Eddowes's throat had been cut, her face mutilated, her abdomen torn open, and her liver and part of her uterus were missing. From marks on one of her fingers, it appeared that one or more rings had been stolen.

The worst was still to come. On Friday, November 9, at 10:45 a.m., the horribly mutilated body of Mary Kelly was found in her own room at 13 Miller's Court, Spitalfields. She had her throat cut, her face all but cut off, her abdomen hollowed out and its contents strewn around her bed, and her heart was missing.

Scotland Yard initiated a huge manhunt to find the murderer, with extra patrols and plainclothesmen scouring the area and detectives questioning hundreds of locals. For one of the first times in police history, careful photographs were taken of the victims and the murder scenes. At the time it was difficult to prove murder without a witness or a confession. These were the days before DNA evidence, before fingerprinting, before CCTV. Investigators did their best, however, going door to door in Whitechapel and hunting up countless leads in more than two thousand interviews. These interviews led to much finger-pointing on the part of suspicious neighbors. Police investigated almost three hundred suspects, including all the neighborhood butchers, and though eighty suspects were credible enough to detain for further questioning, none were ever charged.

The majority of the doctors who examined the bodies held the opinion that the murderer had some anatomical knowledge, and may have used a long, thin surgeon's knife. One interesting fact came out during the investigation of the Chapman murder. Coroner Wynne Baxter, commenting on the missing womb, said that he:

> was informed by the sub-curator of the Pathological
> Museum that some months ago an American had
> called on him, and asked him to procure a number of
> specimens of the organ that was missing in the deceased.
> He stated his willingness to give 20 pounds for each
> specimen, and said his object was to issue an actual
> specimen with each copy of a publication on which
> he was then engaged. He was told that his request was
> impossible to be complied with, but he still urged it,
> saying he wished them preserved, not in spirits of wine,
> the usual medium, but in glycerine, in order to preserve
> them in a flaccid condition, and he wished them sent to
> America direct. It is known that this request was repeated
> to another institution of a similar character.

While most of the suspects were discounted for lack of evidence, there was a growing amount of circumstantial evidence around a certain Dr. Francis Tumblety, who had sailed from the United States to England shortly before the murders began. For a time he had stayed in a first-class hotel in a respectable London neighborhood, but then apparently moved quarters to 22 Batty Street in the East End, right in the center of where the murders were taking place. Tumblety had the money to live better, and the only real reason for him to have moved to such a place was to engage in the various vices on offer in the East End, or for a vice that was particularly his own.

Some of Scotland Yard's records of the investigation have been lost over the years, and the press reports are garbled and occasionally contradictory. One thing that becomes clear, however, is that the police took a great interest in the Batty Street newcomer. He came and went at all hours, and one story is that he left a bloodstained shirt for his landlady to wash. This got him arrested and questioned. He claimed to have cut his hand, and the police released him for lack of evidence. They kept an eye on him, however, and ordered the ports and ships to America to be watched in case he decided to make a run for it.

This wasn't the first time Tumblety had had a run-in with the law. In fact, he had already been arrested in two different countries. Tumblety was born in Canada around 1833, and when he was still young, his family moved to Rochester, New York. Locals remember him as a "dirty, awkward, ignorant, uncared-for, good-for-nothing boy" who sold pornographic books to the crewmen and passengers of the canal boats. He disappeared from Rochester around 1850 and reappeared ten years later, flashing his wealth, wearing expensive and gaudy clothing, and putting on refined airs.

Tumblety had made his fortune selling medicines in the United States and Canada, such as Indian Herbs and the Tumblety Pimple Destroyer. He was generally regarded as a quack, and there's no evidence that he ever got a degree or even much training in medicine. He had to flee St. Johns, New Brunswick, in 1860 when the local coroner declared that one of Tumblety's patients had died because of "atrocious treatment."

During the Civil War, Tumblety moved to Washington, DC, and went around where the officers gathered, trying to impress everyone with his elaborate military costumes and his untrue claims of being a member of General McClellan's medical staff. Despite his blustering nature and his fondness for talking about his talent as a physician, he was a loner and secretive about his personal life, almost never revealing basic details such as where he was born, information about his family, or where he had studied medicine.

He did reveal himself rather too much, however, while hosting a dinner party. In an interview in the December 2, 1888, issue of the *New York World*, Colonel Charles Dunham recalls that during the war he and some other military men accepted Tumblety's invitation to dinner:

> Someone asked why he had not invited some women
> to his dinner. His face instantly became as black as a
> thunder-cloud. . . . He then broke into a homily on
> the sin and folly of dissipation, fiercely denounced all
> women and especially fallen women.
>
> He then invited us into his office where he illustrated
> his lecture, so to speak. One side of this room was
> entirely occupied with doors, outwardly resembling
> wardrobes. When the doors were opened quite a
> museum was revealed—tiers of shelves with glass jars
> and cases, some round and others square, filled with
> all sorts of anatomical specimens. The "doctor" placed
> on a table a dozen or more jars containing, he said, the
> matrices of every class of woman. Nearly a half of
> one of these cases was occupied exclusively with these
> specimens.

When asked why he hated women, Tumblety replied that he had once been married, only to find out that his wife was cheating on him and was a former prostitute. Tumblety's hatred of women was also remembered by a man who acted for a time as his servant.

After failing to make it big in Washington, Tumblety spent the rest of the war in St. Louis and other Missouri cities, still selling his medicines. When John Wilkes Booth assassinated President Lincoln, Tumblety was arrested on suspicion of being part of the conspiracy. It's unclear just why he was suspected, but Assistant War Secretary Charles Dana advised the local judge to put him in jail and force him to tell all he knew about Booth and his associates. The historical record provides no evidence that Tumblety had any part in the assassination. Indeed, he was one of about three hundred people arrested in relation to the crime, the vast majority of them later being released. Was the government simply being overzealous, or was there some connection between Tumblety and the Lincoln assassination that has been lost to time?

So it was this strange figure who was becoming a prime suspect in the Jack the Ripper murders. Chief Inspector John George Littlechild, in a letter written years after the case was closed, said Tumblety, whom he referred to as "an American quack,"

> was at one time a frequent visitor to London and on these occasions constantly brought under the notice of police, there being a large dossier concerning him at Scotland Yard. Although a "Sycopathia [*sic*] Sexualis" subject he was not known as a "Sadist" (which the murderer unquestionably was) but his feelings towards women were remarkable and bitter in the extreme, a fact on record.
>
> Tumblety was arrested at the time of the murders in connection with unnatural offences and charged at Marlborough Street, remanded on bail, jumped his bail, and got away to Boulogne [France]. He shortly left Boulogne and was never heard of afterwards. It was believed he committed suicide but certain it is that from this time the "Ripper" murders came to an end.

The reference to "unnatural offences" most likely refers to homosexual acts, which were illegal and considered mentally aberrant at the time. He was arrested for this at the same time that he was detained for questioning in the Ripper murders a few days after Mary Kelly was killed. While he didn't confess to the more serious crime, police had enough evidence to bring him to trial for moral offenses. He got two acquaintances to post bond for him, and then on November 24, 1888, he sailed to France under an assumed name and then on to the United States.

Scotland Yard wasn't far behind. In fact, they were ahead. London detectives were already waiting for his ship when he disembarked. They'd taken the more direct route from Liverpool, while Tumblety had to go from Boulogne to La Havre before he could catch a ship bound for America. Such extreme measures wouldn't have been taken for a man whom they thought was guilty only of a moral offense, a crime that wasn't even extraditable. The English detectives trailed Tumblety's movements and staked out his apartment building, but on December 6 he disappeared.

London investigators requested samples of Tumblety's handwriting from his San Francisco bank. Presumably this was to compare his handwriting with the many taunting letters to the police signed by Jack the Ripper. There are also reports that Scotland Yard sent investigators to Montreal and New York, both cities where Tumblety spent time.

Despite an extensive search, they never found Tumblety again. Scotland Yard closed the Jack the Ripper case in 1889, stating that the killer had stopped because he had either killed himself or been put in prison or an insane asylum. What they didn't say was that their chief suspect had given them the slip and was still at large in the United States.

Tumblety kept quiet for a time, and his movements are unclear. Soon, though, he began to live more openly and divided his time between Rochester and St. Louis. He developed heart disease and moved into St. John's Hospital in St. Louis for the rest of his days. He died there on May 28, 1903.

An itemized list of his personal effects showed that he kept a large amount of cash in his room (and more in a hefty bank account), some expensive jewelry, and two cheap rings worth only $3. For a man known for his expensive clothing, this last item is odd. Were these the rings taken from Catherine Eddowes, which Tumblety kept as a trophy like so many serial killers do?

The evidence against Tumblety is all circumstantial, as it is for all Ripper suspects, and trying to create a case against him is hampered by the fact that the case files for the investigation are incomplete. Yet the evidence is compelling—his feral hatred of women, the timing of his visits to London, the fact that the murders stopped after he fled, his use of pseudonyms, the rings in his possession, and his knowledge of anatomy. And then there is the fact that Scotland Yard strongly suspected him and sent investigators across the Atlantic to hunt him down. While it will probably never be known whether Tumblety was the world's most notorious serial killer or simply a quack and a con man, his story makes one of the grimmest chapters of Missouri's criminal history.

The Gangs of St. Louis
Prohibition-Era Gangsters

The young thief cursed as he held a bloody handkerchief up to the bullet wound on his face. His friends had carried him to a dingy little backroom in the "Kerry Patch" neighborhood of St. Louis, reassuring him that the doctor would soon arrive, but the Irish-American thug didn't care. His eyes glittered with hatred and determination. No copper's bullet was going to stop Tom Egan. He would rule this neighborhood, him and his gang. He was already the best thief in the area, feared by all. Everyone knew Tom Egan was mean.

And that policeman's bullet had just made him a whole lot meaner.

As the nineteenth century turned into the twentieth, American cities witnessed an unprecedented expansion. The tide of immigrants who had created the country now turned into a flood as quicker and cheaper sea transport made it possible for all but the poorest people to save up enough money for a passage on a steamer. St. Louis and Kansas City, already expanding in the last two decades of the 1800s, boomed as thousands of immigrants, mostly Italian and Irish, came looking for a new life.

Hardworking men and women got jobs as laborers, opened shops, and helped build Missouri into what it is today, but unfortunately these groups brought with them a seedy undercurrent of organized crime. From Ireland came

GETTING READY FOR THE FRAY.

Egan's Rats were also known as "The Indians" for their savage "fixing" of local elections. An early editorial cartoon from the *St. Louis Post-Dispatch* shows that the public was well aware of the gang's political activities.
Courtesy St. Louis Post-Dispatch

hard-drinking brawlers who banded together to form tough gangs. From Sicily came the Mafia, with its rigid codes of silence and vendetta. In Irish and Italian neighborhoods, crime soon became organized, but the fight over who would run it created bloody feuds that lasted for decades.

For the first thirty years of the twentieth century, four gangs dominated St. Louis, two Irish and two Italian, fighting over the stakes in their own neighborhoods but, interestingly enough, rarely facing off against each other and occasionally even cooperating. Organized crime fell along ethnic lines, and their territories encompassed those same lines.

The most notorious of the Irish-American gangs, Egan's Rats, got their name from a policeman (who supplied the "rat" part) and one of their cofounders, Thomas Egan, a hoodlum who grew up in the tough, Irish-American waterfront "Kerry Patch" neighborhood. He and his friend Thomas "Snake" Kinney first formed the gang in the 1890s, picking pockets and committing small-time robberies.

"Snake" Kinney was a pool hustler who decided to get ahead by going into politics. He got elected to the St. Louis Democratic City Committee, helped in no small part by Egan's thugs, who strong-armed people into voting for him and scared opposition voters away. Kinney began moving up the political ladder, losing his rather impolitic nickname in the process, and Egan ended up running the gang all by himself. Kinney became Missouri state senator in 1904 but never cut his ties with his old gangster friend. On the contrary, they remained close all their lives; Kinney even married Tom Egan's sister.

Egan, too, played a role in the rough-and-tumble politics of the era—first using his gang to convince voters to back their favorite candidates for the "Bloody Fourth" ward—and ended up heading the Democratic City Committee. Tom Egan looked every bit as tough as he was. The bullet from that early shootout had left a livid scar on his jaw. Later, in a move that was bold even for him, Egan served as city constable. He kept the peace in his own way, viciously gunning down rivals who tried to operate in his territory and ruling his gang through a mixture of rich rewards and abject terror. Nobody betrayed the Rats while Tom Egan lived.

By the first years of the twentieth century, Egan's Rats had become the most feared gang in the city, killing with impunity, although Egan reassured frightened citizens in an interview with the *St. Louis Post-Dispatch* that "we never shoot unless we know who is present." When one of their members was gunned down and the killer brought to trial, the Rats sought justice in their own fashion by shooting him in the courthouse.

While Egan's Rats were predominantly an Irish-American gang, it was an early equal-opportunity employer. Some Italian immigrants and Jews joined up. If you were vicious enough, you could be a Rat.

Amazingly, Tom Egan died of natural causes in 1919, a rare fate for a St. Louis gangster. His younger brother William took over the gang. "Willie," as most people called him, inherited a complex operation with hundreds of followers. He also inherited a distribution network for liquor. Tom Egan's political savvy made him realize that Prohibition would eventually become the law of the land, so he started building up an underground network of distilleries and distribution centers while alcohol was still legal. Thus when the government banned liquor the year after Tom's death, Egan's Rats were able to step in and supply the demand.

Prohibition was a godsend to the underworld in St. Louis and the rest of the country. Suddenly something a large percentage of the population enjoyed doing had become illegal. Like the prohibition of drugs, the prohibition of alcohol provided a ready and lucrative market for dealers. Hundreds of "speakeasies," as illegal bars were called, opened up overnight, run and supplied by criminal syndicates.

Willie Egan turned out not to be as tough as his big brother and had trouble keeping the Rats together. Soon "Big Maxie" Greenberg, one of the gang's few Jewish members, decided to keep a shipment of bootleg whiskey so he could sell it himself. Willie found out and ordered one of his gunmen to go kill him, but Greenberg was only wounded.

Greenberg joined an up-and-coming group called the Hogan Gang, run by Edward "Jelly Roll" Hogan, the son of a policeman. "Jelly Roll" became a big name in St. Louis bootlegging operations despite holding the post of Missouri State Beverage Inspector. With the large number of gangsters in positions of authority, it's not surprising the law did little to stop bootlegging in particular and gangsterism in general. Only when the body count began to rise and included a growing number of innocent citizens did public outrage grow strong enough to force the government into action. But even the weak attempts to arrest those responsible for the shootings usually came to nothing. There was a conspiracy of silence among gangsters, even when it came to incriminating the other side.

This was eloquently demonstrated by some of Willie Egan's last words. He continued in his attempts to kill Greenberg, but it was Willie who ended up getting gunned down in front of his saloon in 1921. As he lay dying in the hospital, he was asked to identify his killers, but all he said was, "I'm a good sport."

Leadership of the Rats now passed to William "Dint" Colbeck, who was made of tougher stuff than Willie. He had been a member of the Rats since he was old enough to fight, and had served in the Eighty-Ninth Infantry Division during World War I, taking part in the bloody Meuse-Argonne offensive in France. Colbeck had survived poison gas attacks, machine gun fire, and artillery barrages, and wasn't about to be intimidated by the Hogan Gang. He went after them with a vengeance, murdering more than a dozen members and shooting up Hogan's home. After one grand shootout on Lindell Boulevard, in which everyone got away miraculously unscathed, there was a huge public outcry. The gun battles had become too public, too numerous. Colbeck tried to calm the good citizens of St. Louis by telling the *Post-Dispatch:*

> We are not insensitive to the fact that the public is aroused over what the newspapers have consistently characterized as the violence attending the fights between the Hogan and Egan factions. Our men are not trying to disturb peaceful citizens and it is unfair every time violence occurs in St. Louis to attribute it to myself, my men or the rival gang.

This rather self-righteous statement sounds much like the one Tom Egan gave the same paper several years before. What's remarkable about the two interviews is their blatant honesty. The leaders of the Rats had no qualms about admitting they were gangsters or even that they fought running battles with a rival gang. Everyone knew it anyway, so why lie?

Although "Jelly Roll" Hogan survived the several attempts on his life, he lost too many men and was forced to negotiate a truce with the Rats in 1924. Hogan moved on to the greener (and safer) pastures of politics and served four terms in the Missouri State Senate. Egan's Rats were now firmly on top.

Greenberg, slippery as ever, managed to survive the slaughter, making it all the way to 1933 before being found shot dead in a New Jersey hotel.

Whoever Greenberg's killer was, it probably wasn't a member of Egan's Rats. Colbeck, not satisfied with the profits from bootlegging, had started organizing armed robberies. He often went along for the fun, toting a machine gun he had learned to use on German soldiers. It turned out to be just as effective on bank guards. In one famous case, the gang robbed a registered armored mail truck in St. Louis, kidnapping the driver and guard and driving the vehicle to a back alley before emptying the mail pouches. They stole 327 letters containing an undisclosed amount of money. The post office initially claimed that the amount was less than $2,000, but the next day admitted it was more than $70,000 in cash and negotiable bonds. The actual sum turned out to be $2.4 million. The gangsters turned out to be more honest with reporters than the post office was. This and other heists netted the Rats an estimated $4 million.

But this string of armed robberies would be their downfall. Trading in liquor was all well and good, but stealing rich people's money was not something the powers in St. Louis were going to tolerate. State prosecutors got an imprisoned Rat to rat on his fellow Rats. On the basis of his testimony, the courts found Colbeck and eight other gang members guilty of robbing the mail, a federal offense, and gave them twenty-five years each. As Colbeck swapped stories with cellmate Al Capone, the remnants of his gang hid or fled to other cities to join other gangs. Considering their credentials, they had no trouble finding work in the underworld.

Colbeck got out of jail in 1940, having served only sixteen years. He told his parole officer that he had taken a job as a plumber, a trade he learned in his early years, but apparently he once again got embroiled in the politics of the St. Louis mob. Someone shot him dead with a machine gun in 1943.

Prohibition didn't just help Egan's Rats and other Irish-American gangsters. In the Italian neighborhood of the Hill, the men prided themselves on the quantity and quality of the produce from their private stills. Home brewing was an old Italian tradition, and when Prohibition came into force, that hobby became quite profitable. Brewers paid off the cops with cash or free product, and some even got them to help out with the brewing. A few enterprising residents of the Hill lined their cellars with concrete and turned their entire basement into one giant vat. When the St. Ambrose Church burned down in 1921, the rumor went around that the fire started because a vat of moonshine exploded in the rectory.

To keep up appearances, the authorities did conduct a fair number of raids, stopping a tiny percentage of operations by destroying stills and dumping the contents onto the street. Back then it was common for immigrants to keep farm animals to help keep the grocery bill down, and one old-time resident of the Hill recalls that when the booze washed down the street, chickens would drink it up and go wobbling off drunk. Nobody thought to arrest the chickens for consumption of an illegal substance.

While the Hill was rife with bootlegging, it didn't become a center for organized crime like the city's other Italian neighborhood, Little Italy. The Hill was populated mostly by people from Lombardy and east Sicily, regions not known for large amounts of Mafia activity. Little Italy, however, acted as a meeting point for immigrants from West Sicily, the birthplace of the Mafia. It was a cornerstone of West Sicilian society, and it would have been impossible for it not to have been replicated in any West Sicilian neighborhood. While the residents of the Hill were content to brew their own booze and pay off policemen, the gangsters of Little Italy organized into rival operations to run the local liquor trade and extort money from more honest West Sicilians. The Mafia acted like a parasite, living off hardworking Sicilian immigrants who gained their region's bad reputation while seeing none of its rewards.

Organized crime in the Italian neighborhoods of St. Louis had existed as long as there had been a sizeable Italian population there, but things really started getting going when a small group of mafiosi decided to leave Italy in pursuit of their own version of the American Dream. Junior members of the "Green Ones" faction, they had tired of getting the most dangerous jobs while getting the least amount of loot, so they held up a rich theater owner in Palermo to pay their way on a tramp steamer to the New World.

They moved to Little Italy in St. Louis and started their own "Green Ones" away from their old bosses in Sicily. It was a new country, but the same old business. The Green Ones made their living by operating a protection racket, with "clients" given the choice between an informal insurance policy or the wrong end of a shotgun, and when Prohibition passed they added bootlegging to their operations.

In 1923 two police officers named John Balke and Ohmer Hockett discovered one of the Green Ones' stills and decided to make a little extra cash by extorting money from the owner. The bootlegger offered $200, a fair amount at the time, but the police held out for more, so the man told them to wait until his boss arrived. At this point the two cops should have realized they were about to get more than they had bargained for, but they waited patiently until four of the Green Ones showed up. The gangsters proceeded to beat the policemen unconscious, drag them to the woods, dug their graves as they watched, and shot them.

Profits from bootlegging, however, proved too tempting, and soon the Green Ones had competition from another gang, the Cuckoos, who had worked with Egan's Rats to plan the mail truck robbery. The Cuckoos would roar around Little Italy in their cars, each man carrying a Tommy gun. They perfected an early form of drive-by shooting, practicing on leading members of the Green Ones. The gang fought back, and over the next few years dozens would get killed or wounded.

The Green Ones began to fracture under the pressure. Tony Russo, the leader of one of the factions, worried about both the Cuckoos and rival groups among the Green Ones. Russo needed allies. In desperation he turned to Joseph Aiello, a Chicago gangster and rival to Al Capone. The famous gangster still ruled Chicago, and had not yet become Colbeck's cellmate after being found guilty of tax evasion. Aiello offered reinforcements for the battle for St. Louis in return for the killing of one man—Al Capone himself.

Russo went to Chicago with one of his most trusted killers to take care of his end of the bargain, but they got in over their heads. Russo and his henchman were found riddled with bullets.

The war continued and more men on both sides died. In 1928 Tony Russo's brother James was found dead in a vacant lot, alongside the corpse of his henchman Mike Longo. This brought the total number of dead in the war up to twenty-one in a single year. One of the Cuckoos was arrested as a suspect.

James Russo and Mike Longo were buried in Little Italy amidst a throng of mourners and onlookers. Armed policemen walked through the crowd, eyes open to any potential trouble. Patrolmen toting Tommy guns cruised the neighborhood. They even raided the house next door to where Russo lay in an open casket surrounded by $2,000 worth of flowers and wreaths. They had received a tip that some gunmen were plotting to murder the remaining Russos, and they arrested four Italians they found inside. All of them were armed.

That same night the Carr Street police station received a call from Willie Russo, the remaining leader of the Russo faction. He asked the precinct captain for an escort to the train station.

"What for?" the policeman asked.

"I'm leaving town," Willie Russo replied.

"Leaving for good?"

"Yes, for good."

That must have been music to the policeman's ears. He ordered two carloads of heavily armed detectives to escort Willie and his family to the station, where they boarded a train and took off into the night. When speaking with reporters that evening, the police claimed they had no idea what train the Russos had boarded or where they were headed. This was certainly a lie, but while the police may have preferred to see the Russos hunted down and killed, they had offered safe passage out of town, and perhaps hoped that if they honored that promise, more gangsters would take them up on it.

Few did. The gang wars abated for a time, then flared up periodically in the following decades. The Green Ones and Cuckoos had almost wiped each other out in the bid to control the liquor trade, only to lose it in 1933 when alcohol became legal again. Even after that Irish and, increasingly, Italian gangs continued to operate in St. Louis, consuming each other and themselves in a relentless bid for power that continues to this day. But while telling the tales of Prohibition-era gangsters is history, writing about contemporary gangsters is suicide.

The Pendergasts
Running a City Ran in Their Family

It was Election Day in Kansas City in the year 1900. A new century had dawned. For more than a hundred years America's great experiment in democracy had flourished, and now voters once again prepared to freely and fairly elect someone who would honestly reflect the will of the people.

Long lines snaked toward the polling stations, proof of the thriving democratic spirit of the century's first election. But a shrewd observer, or even one not so shrewd, would notice that the lines moved awfully slowly, and that men carried chairs up and down the line, asking people what candidates they intended to vote for. If the answer was acceptable, they got a chair to relax in while they waited. Voters who answered incorrectly had to stand and often ended up leaving in disgust.

And then there were the homeless people, crowded around polling stations in the worst neighborhoods. They seemed content, as if they had just eaten their first big meal in a long time, and they proudly went up to vote for the same slate of candidates the men with chairs supported. When they were done voting, they returned to the back of the line to vote again.

All across the working-class neighborhood of the West Bottoms, drunken mobs poured out of saloons and stumbled to polling stations, convinced by several rounds of free drinks that the saloon owner's candidates were the best men for the job. Not surprisingly, these were the same candidates the homeless people voted for, and the same ones the men with chairs supported. Now if only the drunks could remember the candidates' names . . .

No fear on that score: The saloon owner had men working the polling stations to remind them.

And who was this man? He started life as a nobody, just another working-class Irish American coming to the big city in the hopes of becoming rich and famous. He became both, but not in the usual manner. Like the heroes of other American success stories, he was a shrewd, hardworking businessman who built up a network of important connections, but he was more than that. He was a huckster who rigged elections and virtually ran the Kansas City Democratic Party for decades.

His name was James Pendergast, and he built one of the most successful political machines this country has ever known.

James Pendergast was born in 1856 and grew up in a working-class neighborhood of St. Joseph. Many of his neighbors were Irish Americans like him, but there were also Germans, English, and some African Americans. This eclectic upbringing made him comfortable with a wide variety of people, a skill that would help him in his political career.

In 1876 James, who usually went by "Jim," headed to Kansas City to seek his fortune. Kansas City was a boomtown, acting as the industrial center of the West, and had huge milling and meatpacking operations. The railroad had arrived less than a decade before, and steamboats still chugged down the Missouri River, bringing the city's products to the rest of the world. Pendergast rented a room in a boardinghouse in the crowded West Bottoms, on the Missouri side of the state line. In this raucous neighborhood, working-class families of all ethnicities labored, played, and drank together in crowded but exciting streets lined with saloons and illegal gambling houses. People called the area "the Bottoms" because it sat below a tall bluff called Quality Hill, where the rich lived in giant mansions and frequented the grandiose opera house, the singers doing their best to drown out the sound of the carousing drinkers and churning factories in the Bottoms below.

Pendergast was a muscular, stocky man weighing two hundred pounds, and he had no problem finding a job. At first he worked as a meatpacker in one of the many plants that processed the huge herds that came from as far away as Texas. Then he got a better-paying position as a smelter in an iron foundry before being promoted to the position of puddler, the highly skilled task of pouring molten metal into molds. He made good money, but not enough to satisfy his burning ambition. People didn't come to Kansas City to do well; they came to get rich, and the fine houses on Quality Hill showed him what he could have if he could just figure out how.

Local legend says that he got his first break through sheer luck. Jim had always been a gambling man, and he put a stake down on a long-shot horse named Climax who pulled ahead and won him a pile of money. With it he bought the American House saloon in 1881, in the West Bottoms near the old location for Union Station. A more prosaic theory is that he hoarded his money, working long hours until he could earn enough to make a down payment. Whatever the truth, he had made an excellent choice of businesses. Even though Kansas City had no shortage of saloons, the people never seemed to get enough of them.

The American House also had a boardinghouse and hotel in the same building, which added to his income. The location was good too, right in the center of the red-light "tenderloin" district where men flocked to gamble and meet prostitutes. Jim opened a gaming room in the back of the American House and rented rooms by the hour for any "couples" who didn't need to stay the whole night. He soon had enough money to expand into the building next door. He also set up a banking service to give loans to workers and cash checks. Since many working-class people, especially immigrants, didn't have bank accounts, this earned him a lot of gratitude. Of course he took a small percentage, but that was only to be expected, and his winning personality made people think of him as a friend, not a business owner. Soon everyone knew him as "Big Jim."

Jim now looked set to become one of Kansas City's leading men, but he had other ideas. The snobbish circle of aristocrats and nouveau riche held no interest for him. He stayed in the West Bottoms, where people knew and liked him. He decided a big house on Quality Hill wasn't what he was after. What he really wanted was power.

As an Irish American, the obvious choice was to join the Democratic Party. In 1884 he attended the Democratic City Convention and became one of eleven delegates to represent the Sixth Ward of the West Bottoms.

A bit of political power earned him even more customers, as everyone wanted to get on his good side. Soon his saloon gobbled up more buildings on the 1300 block of St. Louis Avenue, and he brought in many of his younger brothers and sisters to work for him. His brother Tom started coming up from St. Joseph in 1881 when he was only seventeen. Tom liked the excitement and easy money of the big city, and when he was twenty-two he moved there permanently. Tom was much like his brother, a burly man who would be friendly until crossed, and then snapped into a dangerous rage. He worked for Jim as a bartender and was the man to come to if you couldn't see Jim.

Around 1890 Jim bought another saloon, a high-class place right downtown at 520 Main Street. As always, his businesses weren't just for making money but for gaining influence. The new saloon happened to be right near the city hall and the courts, so when influential lawyers or politicians came in to get a drink or engage in a little backroom card playing, Jim would be there with a ready smile and an attentive ear. The savvy lawmakers were probably not fooled by this, but they recognized political talent and ambition when they saw it and made sure to be friendly to him.

From 1887 to 1892 Jim served as a First Ward Democratic committeeman. The First Ward included most of the West Bottoms and pulled a lot of political weight because of all the businesses there. He became well known within the party (and soon across the entire city) for how he handled elections. At this time primaries were done informally by getting people together and having a voice vote. Jim would tell only his friends the time and place for the vote, usually by throwing a free party at his saloon and then getting the drunken crowd to show up at the polling place and scream at the top of their lungs for the candidate of his choice. Whoever got elected knew to whom he owed his office. When more modern techniques were introduced, with supposedly secret ballots, he found that the drunks could be relied upon to do the right thing, and he always had a few other tricks to make sure his candidates won.

Pulling the strings behind his favorite politicians whetted Jim's appetite for more direct power, and he got his large personal following to elect him alderman for the First Ward. Nobody dared oppose him in the primary, and he soundly defeated his Republican opponent in the general election.

Once in office, Jim ran the First Ward much as he ran his saloon—anyone friendly to him and his goals would be treated like gold, and everyone else had better leave. He would get drunks out of jail quickly so they wouldn't lose their jobs, helped policemen who were in trouble with their superiors, gave coal and turkeys to the poor, and basically lent a hand to anyone so that on Election Day he could call in those favors.

High finance in Kansas City at the time was dominated by the small group of white, Anglo-Saxon Protestant businessmen who ran the Commercial Club. This club had no interest in having some grubby Irish saloon owner as one of its members, so Jim merely sidestepped its influence and built a power base of his own. He noticed the club never did any charity work, so he made a name for himself, and made lots of friends, by giving assistance to those in need. Someone who needed a job or some food for their family could always turn to "Big Jim."

He became known as "King of the First" and easily won reelection. He kept his Republican rivals from clamping down on gambling, which was his political cashbox and the main source of income for many of his friends. Although gambling was actually illegal, Jim's friends in the police department gave him protection. They also ran rival operations out of town, making it appear to the public that they were doing something about illegal gambling.

An important aspect of Jim's political job was patronage. Since he got to appoint some posts, and had influence over other politicians who did the same, he could put his own men in the jobs or give contracts to businesses he had invested in. The beneficiaries, of course, would know to whom they owed their allegiance. Patronage was, and still is, one of the ways politicians create a power base.

His little brother Tom worked out well as a bouncer and barkeep, so in 1894 Jim got him a job as a deputy constable in a First Ward city court. Two years later he became deputy marshal in county court. This job paid $100 a month, a lot in those days, but still left Tom with plenty of time to be on committees where he could assert his big brother's interests. Soon Tom became precinct captain, helping Jim cheat on Election Day.

Jim also had another brother, Mike, who helped rig elections but was a bit crazy. He once entered an opposition saloon, bought everyone beer, then threw his own drink in their faces. His political rivals piled onto him and although he got pummeled in the fight, he enjoyed himself thoroughly.

Jim wasn't the only political boss in town, or even in the local Democratic Party. Joseph Shannon moved to Kansas City and had crawled up the ladder of power in a similar fashion to Pendergast. An Irish-American Democrat like "Big Jim," he had his base of support in the Ninth Ward, southeast of downtown.

Pendergast and Shannon started running opposing candidates, and sometimes even allied themselves with the Republicans to beat each other. The origin of their rivalry is unclear; perhaps it was as simple as each not wanting to share the lucrative patronage that came with the jobs.

In the 1900 elections, their greed got the best of them and they spent so much energy fighting each other that the Republicans won several important offices. After this they made a truce such that they fought in the primaries but cooperated in general elections. Their "fifty-fifty" agreement dictated that whoever won, patronage would be split between both factions equally, but of course both sides cheated any chance they could.

One of Jim's best political investments was James A. Reed, a lawyer he and Tom chose to be county counselor, equivalent to the county prosecutor of the modern era. In 1898, backed by Jim's gambling money, Reed won the race for prosecuting attorney in Jackson County. He became mayor in 1900, got reelected 1902, and went on to become senator in 1910.

With such a powerful politician in their pocket, the Pendergasts reaped huge rewards. Reed made Tom Pendergast superintendent of streets, an important job earning $2,000 a year and coming with 250 jobs to hand out as patronage. Jim got to fill 123 police jobs, which made his gambling ring safe from any pesky raids by do-good policemen who actually wanted to enforce the law.

Tom worked out well as superintendent, greatly improving the city streets and gaining public support in the process. He had learned from his big brother that the best way to keep power was to give people what they wanted. He listened to complaints about potholes and litter and treated black neighborhoods and workers the same as white ones, something blacks in Kansas City, or anywhere else in the country for that matter, weren't accustomed to enjoying. In 1902 Tom became county marshal, earning twice his previous salary.

With money rolling in from big government contracts and a wide range of businesses, Jim worked on several charitable projects to improve the quality of life in Kansas City. He organized the building of parks and pedestrian boulevards, assisted by William Rockhill Nelson, a powerful real estate magnate and owner of the *Kansas City Star*. Nelson's paper usually railed against the corruption of the Pendergast family, but Nelson realized that property values would go up with the addition of parks and sidewalks. His paper managed to look the other way while Jim's companies and followers gobbled up the lion's share of building contracts. Apparently Nelson learned something from the Pendergasts about doing well while doing good.

While most of Jim Pendergast's "charitable" projects had ulterior motives, he did seem to have a genuine concern for the people of Kansas City. When the Missouri River overflowed its banks in 1903, displacing hundreds of citizens, Jim provided food and shelter. The good press this generated surely helped him, but in this case at least, he probably spent far more than he earned. He also supported the relocation of Union Station away from the West Bottoms. While this would hurt his saloon business, he saw the new location as more central to the expanded city and in the best interest of the city as a whole.

By the first decade of the twentieth century, Jim's power was at an all-time high, but his health had begun to fail. His beloved wife, Mary, died in 1905, and Jim lost much of his spirit after that. He left his city counsel seat in 1910, a position he had held for eighteen years, and gave it to Tom, who easily won the "election." Jim died the next year.

In the years to follow, Tom Pendergast built up the political machine his brother had founded until he practically ruled

Kansas City. He could make or break politicians, and even helped get an aspiring politician named Harry Truman elected Eastern District judge of the county court, the first step in a political career that would lead to the White House. While Truman tried to distance himself from the Kansas City political machine, in his private papers he referred to Tom Pendergast as "the Boss." When Truman got elected to the senate, many referred to him as "the senator from Pendergast." Not even someone as ambitious as Jim Pendergast could have dreamed that the machine he built would one day reach so high.

But it all came crashing down in 1939 because Tom got too blatant with his election rigging. Times had changed, and the federal government was clamping down on political machines all over the country. Many members of the Missouri Democratic Party saw the Pendergast machine as an embarrassment, opening up the party to accusations of corruption. While nobody could pin any specific corruption on Tom Pendergast, the Treasury Department discovered he had cheated on his taxes and sent him to prison. He only stayed behind bars for fifteen months, but that was long enough for the political machine his brother had built to disintegrate.

In a fitting epitaph, the *Kansas City Times* published an interview with Jim Pendergast on November 11, 1911. Big Jim, in his last months of life, confided, "I've been called a boss. All there is to it is having friends, doing things for people, and later on they'll do things for you . . . You can't coerce people into doing things for you—you can't make them vote for you. Wherever you see a man bulldozing anybody he don't last long."

While his claim that you can't make people vote a certain way isn't exactly borne out by the facts of his career, Jim

Pendergast was right about one thing: One of the only ways to live a life of crime and die a free man is to make more friends than enemies.

The statue of James Pendergast in Case Park, Kansas City. Commissioned by his little brother Tom, it caused an uproar among some of the city's more law-abiding citizens, but it was hard to name another resident who had done more for the city. *Courtesy Missouri Valley Special Collections, Kansas City Library, Kansas City, Missouri*

Young Brothers
Bloody Shootout in the Ozarks

On the cold, overcast afternoon of January 2, 1932, three cars drove along a lonely country road near Springfield in Greene County. Eleven men sat inside, all but one of them officers of the law. They relaxed in their seats, confident the two suspects they planned to arrest would come quietly. They outnumbered the criminals five to one, and brought along revolvers and gas grenades in case of any trouble. The only reason they had such a large posse was because nothing else interesting was going on. They thought it would be a quick, easy catch.

They were wrong, dead wrong.

The officers carried warrants to arrest Jennings and Harry Young for car theft. The brothers had been in and out of jail for various robberies and were especially fond of stealing cars, showing them off to friends and the local girls and selling them when they needed money. Springfield police had arrested the boys' sisters earlier that day when they tried to sell a stolen car to a local auto dealer. The women had confessed that their brothers could be found at the family farmhouse seven miles outside of town. Despite the fact that Harry had been on the run for two years on a murder charge, the officers felt they wouldn't face any trouble.

When they arrived at the Young farm, no one was in sight. The lawmen studied the simple two-story wooden farmhouse with a row of maple trees in the front lawn, and saw no sign of life. They surrounded the house, pounding on the front door and back kitchen door, calling out the brothers' names, and peeking through windows. One of the officers claimed he heard someone walking around inside, but nobody answered their calls.

To soften up any resistance, Detective Virgil Johnson lobbed a gas grenade at an upper-story window, but it only hit the window frame and bounced harmlessly away. Springfield Sheriff Marcell Hendrix decided there had been enough fooling around and went around back with Deputy Wiley Mashburn and Detective Frank Pike. With Hendrix in the lead, they crashed through the door . . .

. . . and right into a shotgun blast.

Sheriff Hendrix took it full in the chest, flying backward, dead before he hit the ground. Mashburn got the next blast in his face and fell next to his boss. Pike, who took the edge of the second blast in the arm, heard a voice inside shout, "Throw down those guns! Come in here or we'll shoot!"

Instead, Pike did the smart thing and sprinted around to the front of the house to warn his friends.

Everyone ducked behind trees or other cover and let loose with their pistols, firing at every window. The Young brothers returned fire, one with a rifle and the other with a shotgun. Johnson got hit in the ankle. He tossed his remaining gas grenade, but it too bounced off a window frame. Within minutes two more lawmen, Detective Sidney Meadows and Patrolman Charles Houser, fell dead with bullets in their heads.

Ollie Crosswhite, a part-time deputy who got paid $2 a day to help patrol downtown Springfield during the shopping season and for other "emergencies," realized he was out of ammunition. He did have a gas grenade, though, so he tossed it. This time the grenade actually made it inside, but the noxious gas didn't slow down the deadly fusillade. The Young brothers were out for blood, and it would take more than gas to stop them. Ducking bullets, Crosswhite crawled toward the back of the house, but the muzzle of a shotgun poked out of a window and blasted into his skull.

Tony Oliver, chief of detectives in Springfield, ordered Johnson and Officer Ben Bilyeau to get to one of the cars and go for help. Both were wounded by this time, and Ralph Wegman, a civilian who had come along just for fun, hurried to join them. They managed to make it without getting shot and sped off toward Springfield.

Oliver's pistol popped away as he hid behind a maple tree, but he was far more exposed than his opponents. Both brothers zeroed in on him, and repeated shotgun blasts ploughed into the tree and tore through the edges of his overcoat. Then a rifle bullet struck his shoulder. Wheeling around, he ran for one of the police cars, but barely got a few feet before a bullet hit him in the back. He staggered on, falling dead just next to the car.

Detectives Frank Pike and Owen Brown, the last men standing outside the house, fled to the barn. They were the fugitives now. Out of ammunition and knowing the Young brothers would soon come for them, they needed to escape, but twenty-five yards of open space lay between them and the cover of a nearby road. It must have seemed like twenty-five miles.

They burst out of the barn, zigzagging across the yard as bullets and shotgun pellets filled the air. Miraculously they got away and hid out until reinforcements arrived.

Johnson and Bilyeau returned within half an hour with more men, as Police Chief Ed Waddle stayed back in Springfield

The posse who came to the Young family farmhouse after the shootout found an eerie scene of bullet-riddled cars and dead patrolmen.
Courtesy City of Springfield, Missouri

frantically calling the National Guard, requesting an artillery battery so he could bombard the house. A vengeful mob formed on the street outside, and soon a long caravan of cars headed out to the Young farm.

Meanwhile, the Young brothers didn't stay idle, although they acted a bit foolishly. They looted their victims' bodies for more guns and hid out near the farm. Even though they had time to run off, something kept them close to the scene of the massacre.

Hundreds of locals showed up, toting hunting rifles or shotguns or no weapons at all. The wail of police and ambulance sirens cut through the excited chatter of voices. Everybody assumed the Young brothers were still inside, so nobody dared approach the house.

Finally two men, Officer Cecil McBride and Sam Herrick, a civilian, crept toward the back of the barn. They heard quiet footsteps and a low voice, then someone whistling for a dog. Sam lost his nerve and hurried back to the others. McBride raised his rifle, had a heart-stopping moment when he realized it was jammed, then pulled out his pistol. A dog started barking and he suddenly saw two men. He immediately opened up and shot Harry Young through the palm of his hand. Jennings Young returned fire with his rifle and McBride ran off, bullets striking the ground all around him.

The lynch mob, oblivious to the gunshots over their own disorganized babble, moved in on the house. They came upon a scene of carnage. Pools of blood and bodies lay scattered across the yard. Remarkably, they discovered Wiley Mashburn still alive by the kitchen door, his face mutilated almost beyond recognition, his left eye hanging out of its socket. An ambulance rushed him to a hospital, but he didn't make it through the night.

Soon the crowd surged inside, and not finding any murderers, took their vengeance out on the house, tearing apart furniture, stealing souvenirs, and trying to set the place on fire. Fortunately, cooler heads prevailed, the fires were tamped out, and the house boarded up until the crime scene could be investigated. The crowd finally did the smart thing and fanned out across the surrounding countryside, but by this point the Young brothers were long gone.

Somehow the fugitives made it seven miles to Springfield and stole a car. It was found the next day in Texas with several of the dead officers' guns inside. Police knew Harry used to hide out in Houston, so they focused their efforts there. Local authorities searched two homes but found nothing. Someone spotted Harry on a bus, but officers arrived too late to catch him.

The Young brothers' faces appeared on every front page in the county, so it wasn't long before details of their movements emerged. Their car had skidded off the road and got stuck in a ditch near Streetman, Texas, at about noon on January 3. A local farmer remembered talking to two male passengers and went off to get a mule team to pull the car out of the ditch. By the time he returned they were gone, having hitched a ride with a traveling salesman. The farmer pulled the car out of the ditch and saw the guns. He also noticed the license plates had been torn off and found them in a nearby field. Suspicious, he called the police. Later the salesman, hearing a description of the two fugitives on the radio, realized he had had a narrow brush with death and called the law.

At this point the Young brothers made a serious mistake. Harry had worked for a time in Houston under the alias Claude Walker, and he went to the house of an old friend to rent a room from him. His new landlord read the papers, however, and the brothers' pictures were in every one. He got his wife and child out of the house and tipped off the police.

This time the cops came prepared, arriving in a posse of a dozen men with tear gas, shotguns, rifles, and machine guns. They surrounded the house and some of the officers burst through the front door. Three officers entered the rented bedroom and saw the door to the adjacent bathroom was closed. One of them tried to open it and ducked out of the way as three shots rang out.

The police responded with an angry volley. After a moment they heard a voice call out, "We're dead, come on in."

The police fired tear gas through the bathroom window before rushing inside to find the brothers lying on the tiles in a widening pool of blood. Jennings was already dead, and Harry dying. It is not entirely clear whether they shot each other in a suicide pact, as the police claimed, or if the police killed them, but both were riddled with gunshot wounds.

It was the end of a long but not terribly successful career in crime. Because they had a similarity in their family name, the Young brothers are often mistaken for descendants of the more famous (and more successful) Younger brothers of the nineteenth century. They were not related and were, in fact, nothing alike. While the Younger brothers served bravely in the Civil War and committed their admittedly bloody crime spree with ability and panache, the more modern Young brothers were little more than incompetent thugs. All the way back in 1918, Jennings and Harry had been charged with breaking into local stores and robbing them, but since it was their first arrest, they only did three years.

That brush with the law didn't teach them a lesson, and soon they graduated to stealing cars. In 1924 Jennings got convicted of breaking into the boxcar of a train and stealing a five-gallon keg of pickles, three rugs, a case of marshmallow candy, and a pail of coconut. Though hardly the stuff of legends, it was enough to get him three years in Leavenworth.

In a twisted sort of sibling rivalry, Harry continued to get in trouble too, being charged with a series of offenses such as handling stolen goods, auto theft, and several burglaries, all in the space of a single year. He got the first three charges dismissed, but went to jail for three years for the last, spending time in a Missouri penitentiary where he met the far more famous outlaw "Pretty Boy" Floyd, also a guest at the institution.

On June 2, 1929, shortly after getting out of jail, Harry got into more serious trouble while driving drunk in the small Greene County town of Republic. A local police officer, Mark Noe, pulled him over. It is unclear what exactly happened next, but it ended up with Harry killing the officer. He fled to Houston under an assumed name.

Meanwhile Jennings got out of jail and promptly got involved in stealing cars again, which had become sort of a family tradition. They kept up that tradition until that fateful winter day in 1932, when they gained the only notoriety they would ever achieve, perpetrating the bloodiest single day for a police force until the terrorist attacks of September 11, 2001.

The Union Station Massacre
The Shooting Spree
That Transformed the FBI

On Saturday morning, June 17, 1933, Union Station was bustling with early morning travelers. People hurried in and out of the station, coming off the trains to visit family or do business in Kansas City, or entering the cavernous waiting hall before heading out to the platform to catch the next train out of town.

Some passengers looked at their watches and frowned. The 7:00 a.m. from Fort Smith, Arkansas, was late, and didn't arrive until 7:15. The train had chugged all night along the Missouri Pacific line through Oklahoma and along the Missouri-Kansas border. As it pulled to a stop, people who wanted to board suddenly had to make way for a tight group of grim-faced men who pushed through the crowd. A worried-looking fellow walked in the center of the group, his wrists handcuffed in front of him. One of the others gripped his belt.

The prisoner was Frank Nash, a convicted bank robber who had escaped from Leavenworth three years before. Guarding him was Joe Lackey, an agent with the relatively new US Department of Justice's Bureau of Investigation, which would later be called the Federal Bureau of Investigation. Frank Smith, another Bureau agent, was with him, along with Otto Reed, a police chief from McAlester, Oklahoma.

Nash himself was nothing remarkable to look at, being a bald, forty-six-year-old man who sported a bright red wig. He'd spent the previous six years in Leavenworth acting like a model prisoner, working his way up through various prison jobs while avidly reading a one-volume set of the complete works of William Shakespeare in the prison library. He became so trusted that he got a job as the deputy warden's chef and handyman. One day the warden sent Nash on an errand outside the prison, and Nash never returned. The complete works of Shakespeare disappeared too.

Just nineteen hours before arriving at Union Station, the trio had swooped down on the unsuspecting fugitive at a store in Hot Springs, Arkansas, hustled him into a car at gunpoint, and sped off. The reason for the style of arrest, which seemed more like a kidnapping, was that Hot Springs was a notorious outlaw hideout where fugitives from the law enjoyed protection by the local underworld. The lawmen had barely gotten out of town before word spread to contacts in the underground network all over the country that one of their own had been taken from their favorite vacation spot.

Local gangsters soon had the agents traced. They had been spotted with Nash at the Fort Smith depot boarding the train to Kansas City. A quick check of the schedule showed when they'd arrive. It didn't take long to arrange a welcoming committee.

Waiting at the station was a second group of lawmen headed by Reed Vetterli, another agent with the Bureau of Investigation. The junior agent that day was Ray Caffrey, who waited anxiously for the job to be over so he could get back to his wife and young son. Accompanying them were two Kansas City Police Department detectives, Bill Grooms and Frank Hermanson, who had arrived in Hot Shot, the department's armored car. Usually Hot Shot came equipped with a submachine gun, but for some reason it was missing that morning.

The local men greeted the train at the platform, and together the seven officers and agents hustled Nash off the train, hemming him in as a tight group. The group kept close order as they crossed the street to Agent Caffrey's car in the parking lot opposite the station. Caffrey put Nash in front. The convict moved to the driver's side so the passenger's side seat could be pushed forward and Lackey, Smith, and Reed could get in back. Hermanson, Grooms, and Vetterli stood on the passenger side talking as Caffrey moved around the car toward the driver's side door.

Then, just in front and a little to the right of the car, someone shouted "Up! Up!"

The lawmen had only an instant to see a man pointing a machine gun at them when another voice shouted, "Let 'em have it!"

At least three machine guns from three different angles opened up simultaneously. Bullets shattered the windows, popped through the metal of the car, and tore through almost everyone. Nash and Reed died immediately, and Lackey writhed in pain as three bullets lodged in his back.

Outside the car, Hermanson, Caffrey, and Grooms fell dead the instant the guns began to fire. A bullet hit Vetterli in the left arm, and he threw himself down as more whizzed by. He crawled to the rear of the car before leaping up and dashing toward the station doors. One of the attackers fired on him, his bullets stitching a ragged line on the stone wall of the station before Vetterli made it safely inside.

The only one left untouched inside the car was Agent Frank Smith. Ducking down below the window, he heard footsteps approach. He slumped over the seat and played possum.

"They're all dead," he heard a voice say. "Let's get out of here."

The gunmen fled, just as Mike Fanning, a Kansas City police officer assigned to the station, came running out to investigate the shots. He fired several times at the gunmen, but missed as they leapt into a car and sped off.

Within moments it was all over. A peaceful, busy train station had become a battlefield, and a stunned calm descended on a scene of carnage that would become known as the Union Station Massacre.

Given the chaos and bloodshed, it's not surprising that eyewitness accounts differ on just about every point. Some people saw two gunmen, some saw up to seven, although most said there were three to five. However many there were, they disappeared into the city. Nobody got a good look at their faces.

J. Edgar Hoover, head of the new Bureau of Investigation, was livid. He took the cold-blooded murder of his agents as a personal affront, and as an opportunity. Eager to give his Bureau additional powers, Hoover used every chance the media gave him to call for tougher federal laws, permission for his agents to carry firearms, and more powers for him and his men. A shocked public and nervous government made sure he got what he wanted.

Hoover told his agents the killers "must be exterminated and they must be exterminated by us."

The Bureau's investigation wasn't helped by the shoddy work done by the police on the scene. Nobody cordoned off the area, and after the initial shock wore off, the parking lot in front of Union Station took on the atmosphere of a carnival. People walked all over the crime scene, smearing the bloodstains and pocketing shell casings as souvenirs while reporters rearranged objects and bodies to take better photographs.

The Bureau scoured the phone records for calls between Hot Springs, Kansas City, and other known gangster hangouts. Soon they had a list of suspects that they slowly narrowed down to three, all of whom the Bureau believed had participated in the shooting.

Phone records pointed to Verne Miller, a local hood in Kansas City. When police searched his home, they dusted for

The bloody scene after gangsters mowed down several lawmen in front of Union Station. Reporters and curiosity seekers tromped all over the crime scene, taking souvenirs and rearranging objects to get better photos. This made it doubly hard for investigators to solve the crime, and the verdict remains controversial to this day.
Courtesy Missouri Valley Special Collections, Kansas City Library, Kansas City, Missouri

fingerprints and came up with a match for Adam Richetti, a known associate of infamous gangster Charles Arthur "Pretty Boy" Floyd, one of the most wanted men in the country. Richetti and Floyd were both in Kansas City at the time and, as friends of Nash and ruthless gunmen, were picked for the job.

After the shooting Richetti and Floyd stayed on the run for a while, but their luck ran out when their car broke down in rural Ohio. Locals thought the men looked suspicious, and when the town's police chief, J. H. Fultz, went to investigate, the men opened up on him. Floyd ran off, but Fultz captured Richetti. He was convicted and went to the gas chamber on October 7, 1938. A posse went after Floyd and gunned him down after a long-running battle.

Miller faced a different sort of justice. His body turned up beside a road outside of Detroit on November 29, 1933. He had been beaten and then strangled to death. The FBI believes he died after an altercation with some other gangster, but perhaps the underworld punished him for his part in the Union Station Massacre. Criminals, after all, don't want to give the cops more reasons to hunt them, and the killings shook up the underworld almost as much as they did respectable society.

Four other gangsters were convicted of conspiracy for their part in planning to free Nash and received the maximum sentence—two years in jail and a $10,000 fine.

The above account is the official FBI version, which stood unchallenged for decades until investigative journalist Robert Unger used the Freedom of Information Act to look at the original files. He found numerous inconsistencies between what agents reported to J. Edgar Hoover and what they said during the Richetti trial. He also found that the Bureau had used strong-arm tactics on some of the witnesses and covered up evidence that one of its own agents had accidentally killed three of the people at Union Station.

His account is as follows.

Hermanson and Grooms, the two local cops, didn't find the machine gun in the Hot Shot, and Unger hints that it might have been taken out to make them more vulnerable. Most of the other agents and officers only had pistols, but Agent Lackey had borrowed a 12-gauge shotgun from the Oklahoma City Police Department before his trip to Arkansas. Chief Reed had his personal 16-gauge sawed-off shotgun. Sometime during the trip they had accidentally switched shotguns. Reed's was of an unusual type and difficult to handle. If not used correctly, it might not fire at all, or it might go off when least expected.

As the agents and officers got into the car, Verne Miller and a second machine gunner approached from the south, facing the front of the vehicle. Lackey saw them coming and fumbled with Reed's unfamiliar gun, trying to get it to shoot, and accidentally blew off Nash's head, one ball bearing continuing on to hit Caffrey. He fired again as the mobsters opened up, but hit Hermanson, and got killed right after that. This idea is supported by the testimony of a cab driver who saw Lackey struggling with a shotgun in the backseat before the firing started.

So some of those dead may have been killed by a fellow lawman. Autopsy reports showed that Ray Caffrey died from a shotgun pellet going through his brain. Doctors found the ball bearing "in or near" his head, and it may have fallen out of the wound as he was dying on the stretcher. In addition, much of Hermanson's skull was torn off as if he too had been killed by a shotgun blast. This testimony was ignored to preserve the reputation of the Bureau.

Unger also disagrees with the list of suspects, and is especially against the idea that "Pretty Boy" Floyd participated in the killing.

Not surprisingly, Unger's account has come under criticism, not the least by the FBI itself. We will probably never know who shot who at Union Station that summer morning back in 1933; all we can say is that the gunfight turned a little-known and almost powerless government bureau into the most famous and effective crime-fighting organization in the world. Before the massacre, agents weren't supposed to carry guns and were restricted to investigating prostitution, interstate car theft, and federal bankruptcy violations. Within a year, they had guns and jurisdiction over virtually all types of federal and interstate crime. The public began to think of the newly renamed FBI as the public's defender against organized crime, the heroes who brought infamous outlaws to justice, dead or alive. Whether the right men were named and killed for the crime doesn't change the fact that the FBI became what it is today because of that bloody morning at Union Station.

Bibliography

Newspapers

Kansas City Star
Kansas City Times
Springfield Daily News
Springfield Leader
St. Louis Globe Democrat
St. Louis Post-Dispatch
St. Joseph Weekly Herald

The Yocum Dollar

Ayres, Artie. *Traces of Silver*. Reeds Spring, MO: Ozark
    Mountain Country Historical Preservation Society, 1982.
Christensen, Lawrence, et al. *Dictionary of Missouri
    Biography*. Columbia: University of Missouri Press, 1999.
Morrow, Lynn. "The Yocum Silver Dollar: Images, Realities,
    and Traditions." In *The German-American Experience in
    Missouri*, 159–76. Edited by Howard Marshall and James
    Goodrich. Columbia: Missouri Cultural Heritage Center
    No. 2, University of Missouri, 1986.
Morrow, Lynn, and Dan Saults. "The Yocum Silver Dollar:
    Sorting Out the Strands of an Ozarks Frontier Legend."
    Gateway Heritage 5 (Winter 1984–85), 8–15.
World Exonumia. Catalog for Mail Bid Sale, September 4, 1984.

The Slicker War

Lay, James H. *A Sketch of the History of Benton County, Missouri*. Hannibal, MO: The Winchell & Ebert Printing and Lithographing Company, 1876.

St. Louis Globe Democrat, July 12, 1896.

Synhorst, Curtis H. "Antebellum Vigilantes: The Slicker War in Missouri." *Gateway Heritage* 3, no. 1 (Summer 1982), 34–48.

Thomas, Clarke, and Jack Glendenning. *The Slicker War*. Aldrich, MO: Bona Publishing Company, 1984.

Vincent, J. W. "The 'Slicker War' and Its Consequences." *Missouri Historical Review* VII, no. 3 (April 1913), 138–45.

William Quantrill

Brownlee, Richard S. *Gray Ghosts of the Confederacy: Guerrilla Warfare in the West, 1861–1865*. Baton Rouge: Louisiana State University Press, 1984.

Christensen, Lawrence, et al. *Dictionary of Missouri Biography*. Columbia: University of Missouri Press, 1999.

Kansas City Star, May 23, 1926.

Leslie, Edward. *The Devil Knows How to Ride: The True Story of William Clarke Quantrill and His Confederate Raiders*. New York: Da Capo Press, 1996.

Yeatman, Ted. *Frank and Jesse James: The Story Behind the Legend*. Nashville, TN: Cumberland House, 2000.

The Other Harry Truman

Brownlee, Richard S. *Gray Ghosts of the Confederacy: Guerrilla Warfare in the West, 1861–1865*. Baton Rouge: Louisiana State University Press, 1984.

St. Joseph Weekly Herald, June 14, 1864.

U.S. War Department. *The War of the Rebellion: A Compilation of the Official Records of the Union and Confederate Armies*. Washington, DC: Government Printing Office, 1888.

Wood, Larry. "Harry Truman: Federal Bushwhacker." *Missouri Historical Review* XCVIII, no. 3 (April 2004), 201–22.

———. *Other Noted Guerrillas of the Civil War in Missouri*. Joplin, MO: Hickory Press, 2007.

Wild Bill Hickok's Springfield Shootout

Miller, F. Thornton. "Wild Bill Hickok, the Springfield Shootout, and the Development of the No-Duty-to-Retreat Doctrine in the Law of the 'Wild West.'" In *Springfield's Urban Histories: Essays on the Queen City of the Missouri Ozarks*. Edited by Stephen L. McIntyre. Springfield, MO: Moon City Press, 2012.

Rosa, Joseph G. *They Called Him Wild Bill: The Life and Adventures of James Butler Hickok*. Norman: University of Oklahoma Press, 1964.

————. *Wild Bill Hickok: The Man and his Myth*. Lawrence: University Press of Kansas, 1996.

————. "Jack McCall, Assassin: An Updated Account of His Yankton Trial, Plea for Clemency, and Execution." *The Brand Book* 32, no. 1 (Winter 1997/1998).

Steward, Dick. *Duels and the Roots of Violence in Missouri*. Columbia: University of Missouri Press, 2000.

Frank and Jesse James

Beights, Ronald. *Jesse James and the First Missouri Train Robbery*. Gretna, LA: Pelican Publishing, 2002.

Brownlee, Richard S. *Gray Ghosts of the Confederacy: Guerrilla Warfare in the West, 1861–1865*. Baton Rouge: Louisiana State University Press, 1984.

Christensen, Lawrence, et al. *Dictionary of Missouri Biography*. Columbia: University of Missouri Press, 1999.

Croy, Homer. *Last of the Great Outlaws: The Story of Cole Younger*. New York: Duell, Sloan and Pearce, 1956.

Kansas City Times, September 27 and 29, 1872, and October 15 and 20, 1872.

Koblas, John. *The Great Cole Younger and Frank James Historical Wild West Show*. St. Cloud, MN: North Star Press of St. Cloud, 2002.

Parrish, William. *A History of Missouri. Volume III: 1860 to 1875*. Columbia: University of Missouri Press, 1973.

Settle, William A. *Jesse James Was His Name*. Columbia: University of Missouri Press, 1966.

Stiles, T. J. *Jesse James: Last Rebel of the Civil War*. London: Vintage Books, 2002.

Yeatman, Ted. *Frank and Jesse James: The Story Behind the Legend*. Nashville, TN: Cumberland House, 2000.

Cole Younger

Beights, Ronald. *Jesse James and the First Missouri Train Robbery*. Gretna, LA: Pelican Publishing, 2002.

Christensen, Lawrence, et al. *Dictionary of Missouri Biography*. Columbia: University of Missouri Press, 1999.

Croy, Homer. *Last of the Great Outlaws: The Story of Cole Younger*. New York: Duell, Sloan and Pearce, 1956.

Koblas, John. *The Great Cole Younger and Frank James Historical Wild West Show*. St. Cloud, MN: North Star Press of St. Cloud, 2002.

Parrish, William. *A History of Missouri. Volume III: 1860 to 1875*. Columbia: University of Missouri Press, 1973.

Yeatman, Ted. *Frank and Jesse James: The Story Behind the Legend*. Nashville, TN: Cumberland House, 2000.

Younger, Cole. *The Story of Cole Younger by Himself*. St. Paul: Minnesota Historical Society Press, 2000.

———. *What Life Has Taught Me*. Typescript speech preserved in the Western Historical Manuscript Collection, University of Missouri-Columbia.

Belle Starr

Christensen, Lawrence, et al. *Dictionary of Missouri Biography*. Columbia: University of Missouri Press, 1999.

Croy, Homer. *Last of the Great Outlaws: The Story of Cole Younger*. New York: Duell, Sloan and Pearce, 1956.

Shirley, Glenn. *Belle Starr and Her Times: The Literature, the Facts, and the Legends*. Norman: University of Oklahoma Press, 1982.

Younger, Cole. *The Story of Cole Younger by Himself*. St. Paul: Minnesota Historical Society Press, 2000.

The Bald Knobbers

Christensen, Lawrence, et al. *Dictionary of Missouri Biography*. Columbia: University of Missouri Press, 1999.

Groom, Charles, and D. F. McConkey. *The Bald Knobbers, or Citizen's Committee of Taney and Christian Counties, Missouri*. Forsyth, MO: Groom & McConkey, 1887.

Hartman, Mary, and Joe Ingenthron. *Baldknobbers: Vigilantes on the Ozarks Frontier*. Gretna, LA: Pelican Publishing Company, 1988.

Spencer, Thomas. "The Bald Knobbers, The Anti-Bald Knobbers, Politics, and the Culture of Violence in the Ozarks, 1860–1890." In *The Other Missouri History: Populists, Prostitutes, and Regular Folk*, 31–49. Columbia: University of Missouri Press, 2004.

Did Jack the Ripper Live in St. Louis?

Evans, Stewart, and Paul Gainey. *The Lodger: The Arrest and Escape of Jack the Ripper*. London: Century, 1995.

Jakubowski, Maxim, and Nathan Braund. *The Mammoth Book of Jack the Ripper*. London: Constable & Robinson Ltd., 2008.

Riordan, Timothy B. *Prince of Quacks: The Notorious Life of Dr. Francis Tumblety, Charlatan and Jack the Ripper Suspect*. Jefferson, NC: McFarland & Company, Inc., 2009.

The Gangs of St. Louis

Kefauver, Estes. *Crime in America*. Garden City, NY: Doubleday and Co., Inc., 1951.

May, Allan. "The St. Louis Family," Crime Library website. www.crimelibrary.com/gangsters_outlaws/family_epics/louis/1.html (accessed February 5, 2008).

Mormino, Gary. *Immigrants on the Hill: Italians in St. Louis, 1882–1982*. Columbia: University of Missouri Press, 2002.

St. Louis Post-Dispatch, April 2 and 3, 1923, and July 29 and 30, 1928.

Waugh, Daniel. *Egan's Rats: The Untold Story of the Gang That Ruled Prohibition-era St. Louis*. Nashville, TN: Cumberland House, 2007.

The Pendergasts

Christensen, Lawrence, et al. *Dictionary of Missouri Biography*. Columbia: University of Missouri Press, 1999.

Dorsett, Lyle. *The Pendergast Machine*. Lincoln: University of Nebraska Press, 1968.

Larsen, Lawrence, and Nancy Hulston. *Pendergast!* Columbia: University of Missouri Press, 1997.

McLear, Patrick. "'Gentlemen, Reach for All': Toppling the Pendergast Machine, 1936–1940." *Missouri Historical Review* XCV, no. 1 (October 2000), 46–67.

Reddig, William. *Tom's Town: Kansas City and the Pendergast Legend*. Columbia: University of Missouri Press, 1986.

Young Brothers

Barrett, Paul and Mary. *Young Brothers Massacre*. Columbia: University of Missouri Press, 1988.

Davis, Bruce. *We're Dead, Come on In*. Gretna, LA: Pelican Publishing Company, 2005.

Springfield Daily News, January 3–14, 1932.

Springfield Leader, January 3–14, 1932.

The Union Station Massacre

Clayton, Merle. *Union Station Massacre: The Shootout That Started the FBI's War on Crime*. New York: The

Bobbs-Merrill Company, 1975.

"Famous Case: Kansas City Massacre—Charles Arthur 'Pretty Boy' Floyd." Federal Bureau of Investigation website. www.fbi.gov/libref/historic/famcases/floyd/floyd.htm (accessed December 12, 2007).

Unger, Robert. *The Union Station Massacre: The Original Sin of J. Edgar Hoover's FBI.* Kansas City, MO: Andrews McMeel Publishing, 1997.

Index

Index

Index

Index

Index

About the Author

Sean McLachlan first came to Missouri in the 1990s to earn a master's degree in archaeology at the University of Missouri-Columbia and fell in love with the rich heritage of the state. He worked for ten years as an archaeologist in Israel, Cyprus, Bulgaria, and the United States before earning a second master's at the University of Missouri's School of Journalism. McLaclan is now a full-time writer, and his work has appeared in such publications as *Missouri Life*, *British Heritage*, and *Ancient Egypt*. He is the author of numerous books, including *It Happened in Missouri* (published by TwoDot Press) and the novel *A Fine Likeness*, set in Civil War Missouri. Visit him on the web at midlistwriter.blogspot.com.